TOP VISIONARIES
WHO CHANGED THE WORLD

George Ilian

Published by Bright & Happy Books, LLC
Libertyville, IL 60048

Top Visionaries Who Changed the World
LC Control Number: 2018944518

ISBN 978-1-946477-06-4

Manufactured in the United States of America

MV 10 9 8 7 6 5 4 3 2 1

Contents

WELCOME

What if you could sit down to dine with some of the world's most successful entrepreneurs and have a conversation with them? What would you ask them? What business ideas and life lessons would they give to you? Of course, it's not possible to deliver any one of these rock-star entrepreneurs to your dinner table—no matter who's doing the cooking or what you're serving.

But I could be your ambassador, and in this book I will present you with eight of the world's greatest contemporary visionaries, people who have truly changed the way we live and think, the way we work and play, the way we see the world itself. Some might even be controversial and show us some bad examples to learn from. One thing I've learned over my years of entrepreneurship is that if you don't have passion for the business you are doing, the probability of making it is very low. I'm here to fuel that passion by giving you some great ideas you can depend on.

The goal is to get you motivated and inspired to take action and succeed in life. I was inspired to start working for myself and be my own boss after I read Richard Branson's biography, and one on Steve Jobs really made me want to be the best at what I do. But reading these long books, more than 500 pages each, is really time-consuming, so I put the most important information about each person into a short, digestible form so you can get the most value in the shortest period of time. You will learn the most important things about each person, they will get you motivated, and they will save you time!

This book is by no means encyclopedic, but it is not intended to be. The chapters progress chronologically and in bite-size chunks, so that you can dip in and learn about a specific period in an entrepreneur's life, a particular project, or a certain achievement. We cannot all become a Mark Zuckerberg or found a company as game-changing as Facebook, but we can make the most of his example and become ever more successful in the things we do.

So how were these eight people chosen? To a large extent by their impact. How original were their ideas? How influential did they become? Did they transform our personal lives in any significant way? Did they alter our professional lives to allow us to become more productive, more thoughtful, or better equipped to accomplish things to make our own mark in the world? Admittedly, the answers to these questions are entirely subjective. As are the choices of the people in this book, all of them world-changers whose products and services have found their way into our lives. And just as important as what these visionaries have brought to the world are their deserved reputations for building workplaces that encourage creativity, innovation, and meaning.

The goal here is to bring each person's experience and wisdom to these pages for your benefit, to inspire you so you can learn and achieve. I want this book to be both a meditation on entrepreneurship and an inspiration for those who want to create something meaningful on their own. There is much more similarity than difference in the ways these people think. They all start out not thinking about themselves; they begin thinking externally about how they can help their country (and even the world).

Every successful entrepreneur shares the following assets: an opportunistic mindset, an acceptance of risk and potential failure, and independence and control. Let me explain.

Opportunistic Mindset

Where others see disruption and chaos, entrepreneurs see opportunity. It is a simple, even romantic notion of entrepreneurship, perhaps, but still, many great businesses have been created by people who were able to clearly spot an opportunity in the chaos of a crowded marketplace.

Acceptance of Risk and Potential Failure

While entrepreneurs are far more willing than the average person to assume the necessary risk that comes with creating something new, they are just as ready to allow for the possibility that they could be wrong—dead wrong at times. Among venture capitalists, in fact, failure is viewed as something like a badge of honor because you learn way more from your failures than from your successes.

Independence and Control

Almost everyone wants to have a sense of independence and control over their life. But with entrepreneurs, having these is as much a need as a want. Steve Jobs is a great example in how he took control of his customers' full user experience, from the buying through the packaging to the hardware and software. Make no mistake about it: The need for control is fundamental to an entrepreneur's vision. Individuals with an external focus of control typically believe that events happen as a result of circumstances that are beyond their control. By contrast, people who possess internal focus of control believe that the events in their life result directly from their own actions or behavior.

To these three core stances, entrepreneurs bring drive, tenacity, and persistence. They live what they believe, building success through a strong culture and values. They seek out niches and market gaps. They are the architects of their own passionate and focused vision. An often common though little-noticed trait among many of the most successful entrepreneurs is personal tragedy. For example, Winfrey was sexually abused as a child, but she still had the will to overcome every obstacle. This strength comes from their trust in themselves, so many of these entrepreneurs share a fundamental adversity. If there is turmoil in their lives, there seems to be a vision to move far beyond it.

All of these traits and challenges are evident in the following introductions to some of the world's greatest entrepreneurs. These exceptional institution builders offer a treasure chest of insights: how to seize new opportunities, build valuable and lasting companies, lead people, think more creatively, and overcome obstacles. All of them know how to win. All of them are winners.

This book will stimulate your thinking and help you make the necessary adjustments needed to ensure success in your situation. I hope these ideas will provide you with the inspiration to learn more or develop your thinking along new, creative lines and generate brilliant ideas for your life and your business.

Steve Jobs

INTRODUCTION

To many people, the slightly built, graying, bespectacled gentleman in a long-sleeve black turtleneck and blue Levi's jeans would never have warranted a second look. Steve Jobs was extraordinary in his apparent ordinariness.

When you peel back the layers, however, he was far from ordinary. His far-sightedness, persistence, and absolute faith in the Apple brand and products catapulted the company out of nowhere in 1976 to global superstar status today: Apple is the world's largest publicly traded corporation, and in 2015 it became the first American company ever to be valued at more than $700 billion. If you want to understand Apple, you need to think big. If, like Jobs, you want to conceive a success story like Apple's, you need to have the unrestricted imagination and ambition to think even bigger than that.

The birth and rebirth of Apple were by no means Jobs's only achievements. He transformed the world of consumer technology, not only in computing but in music and digital animation, too. He brought lines of previously inconceivable products to the marketplace, sold those products direct to consumers, and made computing cooler than it had ever been before. He has quite rightly been acclaimed as the entrepreneur, and the CEO, of his generation and one of the greatest innovators of all time.

A MAVERICK IS BORN

Steve Jobs was born in San Francisco on February 24, 1955. His biological parents, Syrian-born Abdulfattah "John" Jandali, a graduate student at the University of Wisconsin, and Joanne Carole Schieble, a Swiss American undergraduate, weren't planning on parenthood so soon; and even after Schieble became pregnant, her conservative father refused to let the pair marry. They gave their son up for adoption as soon as he was born, and he was taken in by Paul and Clara Jobs, who had been married since 1946 but were unable to conceive children. Schieble had specified that the baby should be adopted only by college graduates, but although the Jobses both had relatively little formal education, a compromise was struck when they promised to encourage, and financially support, the child through university.

 Your start in life is not what's most important. It's where you end up that counts.

Jobs did not share the concerns many adopted children have about their families; he believed he was not abandoned by his birth parents but rather chosen by his adoptive ones, stating that Paul and Clara Jobs "were my parents 1,000 percent." Jobs's authorized biography by Walter Isaacson quotes him as reiterating, "Paul and Clara are 100 percent my parents. And Joanna and Abdulfattah are only a sperm and an egg bank. It's not rude, it is the truth." The Jobses lavished affection on their adopted son and provided him with a comfortable, stable childhood.

When Jobs was five, the family moved to Mountain View, California, which would later become the heart of Silicon Valley, and shortly after the move, Paul and Clara adopted a daughter, Patty. The Jobs family was complete, and Steve's childhood was stable and unremarkable. His mother worked as an accountant for Varian Associates, one of California's first high-tech firms, and his father worked as a mechanic and carpenter. Young Jobs was encouraged to work alongside his father in the workshop, where he picked up many practical skills. He learned how things function and how to make them with his own hands. The Jobses were unpretentious, practical people and passed their work ethic on to their children.

Jobs was a smart child, scoring two grades higher than his age group on elementary-school tests, but he didn't exactly apply himself and was often disruptive in class. He skipped a year of school, and while at Homestead High School in Cupertino, California, he forged a close friendship with Bill Fernandez, who later became Apple's first employee. Fernandez introduced Jobs to his neighbor, Steve Wozniak. Together, Jobs and Wozniak would transform the world of technology.

> **"I just think he [Gates] and Microsoft are a bit narrow. He'd be a broader guy if he had dropped acid once or gone off to an ashram when he was younger."**
>
> —STEVE JOBS

Jobs graduated from high school in 1972 and, true to his parents' promise, they enrolled him at Reed College in Portland, Oregon, despite being ill-equipped financially to do so. Jobs lasted just six months at Reed before dropping out. He slept on friends' dorm-room floors, recycled Coca-Cola bottles to earn a few cents, and ate free meals at a Hare Krishna temple. This could well have been the end of Jobs's story, but just because he had no interest in conventional education didn't mean he'd be a lifelong underachiever.

The same year, Wozniak designed and built a new version of the iconic arcade game *Pong*, and he asked his friend Jobs to present it to Atari, Inc. at its head office. Thinking Jobs was the creator, Atari offered him a job as a technician, and Jobs did not dissuade them of their view. He worked for the company during the early 1970s and took a seven-month sabbatical to India, where he stayed at an ashram and sought spiritual enlightenment from a variety of religious teachers. He studied Zen Buddhism seriously, considered becoming a monk at the Eihei-ji temple in Japan, and remained a practicing Buddhist throughout his life.

Jobs's travels in this period had a profound effect on him. When *Wired* magazine in 1996 asked about the importance of gaining a variety of experience, he said: "Unfortunately, that's too rare a commodity. A lot of people in our industry haven't had very diverse experiences. So they don't have enough dots to connect, and they end up with very linear solutions without a broad perspective on the problem. The broader one's understanding of the human experience, the better design we will have."

 Be open to new experiences.

Jobs was adamant that his cross-cultural experiences as a young man in India and his countercultural values were essential to the development of his thinking. He believed that unless you shared those experiences and values, you would not be able to relate to him. Right from the beginning, Jobs wanted to be seen as an outsider, a rebel, and a maverick.

When Jobs returned to the U.S. after his sabbatical, he and Wozniak worked on more arcade games for Atari and also on blue-box telephone-dialing devices designed to circumvent long-distance tolls. In both cases, their focus was on reducing the number of chips used in the circuit-board design to make them cheaper to manufacture. The pair experimented with different technologies and sold their blue boxes illegally. Computing as a discipline was in its earliest phase in the mid-1970s, and both Jobs and Wozniak joined the Homebrew Computer Club in Menlo Park, California, a group of technically minded individuals who met, experimented, chatted, and traded parts as a hobby. It was at the first Homebrew meeting that Jobs saw an MITS Altair, one of the earliest microcomputers, and Wozniak subsequently recalled that at that moment he was inspired to design the first Apple product.

THE BIRTH OF APPLE

Jobs may be the famous face of Apple, but there's a strong case that Wozniak was the brains of the outfit, at least in the company's earliest phase. Inspired by the electronics samples he and Jobs had seen at the Homebrew Computer Club, Wozniak built the Apple I personal computer kit, a preassembled circuit board. Users had to add their own monitor, power supply, and keyboard, and the Apple I had just 4KB of memory.

Even if Wozniak was the technical whiz kid, Jobs was the one with a head for figures and who saw the commercial value of Wozniak's invention. Jobs obtained the first order, for 50 machines, from the Byte Store, a local computer outlet in Mountain View. The order was worth $25,000, and the parts alone cost $20,000; since the components had been bought on 30-day credit, all 50 had to be built and delivered to Byte within 10 days. The Apple I went on sale in July 1976, and a single unit cost $666.66 (equivalent to $2,763 today).

 Know your strengths and those of the people around you.

Apple was incorporated as a company in January 1977, by which time the Apple I was selling well. The sole shareholders were Jobs and Wozniak, who had bought out a third partner, Ronald Wayne, for $800. Wayne was older and, unlike his cofounders, had personal assets and found the venture too risky, though he'd come to rue his premature exit. If Wayne had kept his 10 percent stock until February 2015, when Apple's value exceeded $700 billion, it would have been worth approximately $60 billion.

To grow the company while allowing Wozniak to develop new products, Jobs had to take responsibility for raising substantial funding. He convinced Mike Markkula, an angel investor who had made his own fortune from stock options he acquired working at Intel, to provide an equity investment of $80,000 and an additional loan of $170,000. In exchange, Markkula took one-third of Apple's shares and became employee No. 3. He was a trained engineer and brought both experience and credibility to the new company. He wrote programs for the Apple II, beta-tested products, introduced Michael Scott as Apple's first CEO and president, and helped Jobs obtain additional venture capital. Jobs was humble enough to recognize his own limitations, watch Markkula attentively, and learn from him. For Jobs, Markkula was both a business partner and a mentor, and this period in the late 1970s was probably the most important period of education in Jobs's life.

Apple's second project, the not-so-imaginatively named Apple II, debuted in April 1977; unlike the Apple I, it had a commercial launch at the West Coast Computer Faire. It was light-years ahead of its competitors for three reasons: The Apple II had cell-based color graphics, it was based on open architecture, and you could use a regular cassette tape for storage. Later versions could take a 5.5-inch floppy disk instead of a cassette tape, and a custom-built interface called Disk II was created for it. The Apple II was one of only three computers on the market to be released specifically for home users. Collectively these three were known as the 1977 Trinity; the other two were the Commodore PET and the Tandy Corporation's TRS-80.

The first computer spreadsheet program, VisiCalc, was released in the middle of 1979 by Software Arts. It was one of the first pieces of truly user-friendly software. It retailed for under $100, and, most important, for the first 12 months it was available, it was compatible only with the Apple II. Some users bought the Apple II specifically to run VisiCalc, and the machine ceased being a novelty item for tech geeks and became an essential part of the office furniture. Apple made the transition into the business market without having to make changes to its product or spend a fortune on advertising.

Apple's growth accelerated through the late 1970s. Jobs ran a professional team, from the computer designers to the workers on the production line, and together they studied how to utilize existing products and ideas in innovative ways. Jobs took his team to Xerox PARC, a research-and-development company in Palo Alto, California, in December 1979. Here they first saw Xerox's graphical user interface (GUI), and Jobs was adamant that this was the future of computing. He negotiated three days' use of Xerox's facilities in exchange for $1 million of pre-IPO stock, and that was all the time his team needed to dream up the core features of the Apple Lisa, the first personal computer with a GUI to be aimed at individual business users. Xerox undoubtedly did well out of this deal too: The pre-IPO price it negotiated was just $10.

Apple had a bumper crop in 1980: Jobs launched the Apple III in May, and the company received attention-grabbing coverage in both *Kilobaud Microcomputing* (the leading magazine for computer hobbyists) and *Financial Times*, so on December 12, 1980, Apple launched its initial public offering. This immediately created 300 millionaires (more than any other company in history) and raised more capital than any U.S. firm since the Ford Motor Company in 1956. The market was buzzing, and investors and commentators alike wanted a slice of the Apple pie. The opening share price was $22, so Xerox instantly made a fortune, as did many other venture capitalists who had backed the company in its earliest days.

Apple's first shareholder meeting as a public company took place in January 1981. Jobs took to the floor with a preprepared speech, but he shortly abandoned his script and spoke from the heart. Investors bought into the Jobs brand, and Apple's, because Jobs's charisma and passion for his products spoke volumes. He exuded a confidence others found irresistible. Later—as when he enticed Mike Scott to join Apple from National Superconductor in 1978—when Jobs reached out to John Sculley (then president of Pepsi Cola) to become Apple's CEO in 1983, Sculley wouldn't have dreamed of refusing. Jobs knew having the right team at Apple was the key to its long-term success, and he wasn't afraid to tell people so.

> **"My model for business is the Beatles. They were four guys who kept each other's kind of negative tendencies in check. They balanced each other, and the total was greater than the sum of the parts."**
>
> —STEVE JOBS

The Macintosh

The product that put Apple on the map in the company's formative years was the Macintosh, the first mass-produced personal computer with an integral GUI and a computer mouse to control it. The Macintosh took its name from Apple designer Jef Raskin's favorite kind of apple (the McIntosh), but as another company (McIntosh Laboratory, Inc.) already owned that name and refused to give Jobs a release for it, the spelling change was necessary. Jobs was emotionally attached to the Macintosh, as were many members of its development team. He told *Playboy* magazine in 1985, "I don't think I've ever worked so hard on something, but working on Macintosh was the neatest experience of my life. Almost everyone who worked on it will say that. None of us wanted to release it at the end. It was as though we knew that once it was out of our hands, it wouldn't be ours anymore. When we finally presented it at the shareholders' meeting..., I could see the Mac team in the first few rows.... Everyone started crying."

When Jobs was working on the Macintosh, his colleague Bud Tribble coined the phrase *reality-distortion field* (RDF) to describe his boss's ability to convince himself (and everyone else) that what seemed to be impossible was in fact possible. Jobs used a mixture of charisma, bravado, hyperbole, and dogged persistence to get his message across, though critics have suggested he sometimes allowed the distortion of reality to run too far. Even though his colleagues were aware of it, they easily fell into the RDF—this was how inspirational and motivational Jobs was as a leader of his team.

The public product launch of the Macintosh was second to none. Apple spent $2.5 million buying all 39 advertising pages in a special edition of *Newsweek*, inserted an 18-page brochure into numerous other magazines, and paid $1.5 million for its now legendary "1984" commercial, directed by future Oscar nominee Ridley Scott, to air on the Super Bowl broadcast. Parodying scenes from George Orwell's dystopian novel *1984*, the ad's heroine wore a Macintosh T-shirt, and together, woman and company saved the world from conformity. The response from Apple's shareholders was ecstatic.

 Build and sell great products that you believe in.

The Macintosh went on sale two days later, and Apple ran a "Test Drive a Macintosh" promotion, a new idea whereby anyone with a credit card could borrow a computer for 24 hours to try it out at home. Far in excess of Apple's predictions, 200,000 consumers participated, and demand was so high that Apple couldn't make machines fast enough to meet it. Apple increased the price from $1,995 to $2,495, but consumers still flocked to the stores.

The GUI on the Macintosh was completely new, so in order to avoid its product being labeled a novelty item, Apple had to develop new software to work with its platform. Apple bundled two programs with the Macintosh (MacWrite and MacPaint), encouraged Microsoft and Linux to develop Mac-compatible versions of their software, and launched its own Macintosh Office package before the end of 1985. These moves were Apple's first ventures into software, but Jobs recognized that his machines would never dominate the market unless there were sufficient high-quality programs to run on them.

Although Jobs was charming and persuasive, he was also disorganized and erratic in his management style. Colleagues remember Jobs running meetings into the early hours of the morning and then still expecting staff to be at their desks at seven A.M. This inevitably caused tension in the office, particularly with newly appointed CEO John Sculley. The working relationship between the two men soon deteriorated. Jobs attempted to oust Sculley but failed, and the move backfired terribly: Apple's board of directors gave Sculley the authority to remove Jobs from all posts except chairman, and they stripped Jobs of his managerial duties, too. He stopped coming to work and resigned completely five months later.

THE NeXT STEP

Bruised from his ignominious departure from Apple, which had been the dominant feature in his life for the previous decade, Jobs toyed briefly with the idea of crossing the Iron Curtain and opening a computer company in the USSR. He also applied (unsuccessfully) to become a civilian astronaut on board the International Space Station. With the commercial responsibility of Apple lifted from his shoulders, Jobs became happier and more creative: In a commencement speech at Stanford University in 2005 he looked back on his firing from Apple as the best thing that could possibly have happened to him, reflecting, "I'm pretty sure none of this would have happened if I hadn't been fired from Apple. It was awful-tasting medicine, but I guess the patient needed it."

 Stay hungry, stay foolish, look critically at yourself, know your mistakes, and work hard to fix them.

Jobs had sold all but one of his 6.5 million Apple shares and consequently pocketed $70 million, an eye-watering sum at any point in history but especially in 1985. The first thing he did was to invest $7 million of his own money into a new venture, NeXT, partnering with billionaire investor Ross Perot. Jobs used the expertise he had gained from Apple, but, crucially in this new company, where he alone made the decisions, he could take the products in the direction he wanted to. He had ideas about architecture he wanted to pursue, so he set off and tried them out.

Priced at $9,999, the first NeXT computer was too expensive for the home and education users it had originally been designed for. It did, however, contain experimental technologies, such as digital signal-processor chips, a built-in Ethernet port, and a Mach operating-system kernel; these innovative features made it attractive to the financial, scientific, and academic communities. Jobs identified this interest and galvanized the media to cover the gala event that marked the product's launch. His hunch that the NeXT was best suited as a research machine was right: Tim Berners-Lee invented the first web browser on his NeXT workstation. Following his hunches was important to Jobs, and more often than not they proved correct.

Jobs was not satisfied with the first version of NeXT, so in less than a year he released the NeXTcube, advertising it as the first "interpersonal" computer: a personal computer you could use to share voice files, images, graphics, and video by email. This had never been possible before. Jobs told reporters that this marked a revolution in computing, and in many ways this was true. Journalists picked up the message and ran with it.

In the development of the NeXTcube, we first see Jobs's obsession with aesthetics, a major factor in Apple's later success. He described his philosophy as follows: "When you're a carpenter making a beautiful chest of drawers, you're not going to use a piece of plywood on the back, even though it faces the wall and nobody will see it. You'll know it's there, so you're going to use a beautiful piece of wood on the back. For you to sleep well at night, the aesthetic, the quality, has to be carried all the way through."

Much to the horror of NeXT's hardware department, Jobs demanded that the NeXTcube be given a magnesium case. This was not only more expensive but more difficult to work with than earlier plastic cases. Jobs won the argument by force of personality, and from then on he has always been associated with products that are as visually appealing as they are functional.

 Do what you believe is right, even if it doesn't make sense to others at the time.

Jobs understood from his experience with the Macintosh that users wanted first-rate software to run on their new machines, and he encouraged software developers to design NeXT-compatible programs. The machines came preinstalled with Mathematica (a program for those working in the scientific, engineering, mathematical, and computing fields), and by the early 1990s a number of computer games became available for

NeXT machines, including *Doom, Heretic,* and *Quake.* You could install the Merriam-Webster Dictionary and the complete works of Shakespeare, too, should you feel so inclined.

NeXT computers at first had their own proprietary operating system, NeXTSTEP, but within a year of the brand's launch, Jobs realized it was the operating system, not the hardware, that would make NeXT a fortune. He took the bold step of reorienting the company's business strategy. He oversaw the development of a PC-compatible version of NeXTSTEP in 1991, held a demo of it at the NeXTWorld Expo in January 1992, and by the middle of 1993 the software was selling well to corporate clients. Industry trendsetters such as Chrysler, First Chicago, NBC, and the Swiss Bank Corporation, as well as government bodies, including the Central Intelligence Agency, the National Security Agency, and the Naval Research Laboratory, installed the operating system. Their belief in the software encouraged others to follow suit.

Under Jobs's leadership, NeXT stopped making hardware completely in 1993 and concentrated on software alone. Sun Microsystems invested $10 million in NeXT, and together Jobs and Sun's CEO, Scott McNealy, built a new operating system called OpenStep, a version of which was available for Microsoft Windows. More important than this, however, was their launch of WebObjects, a platform for building large-scale dynamic web applications. This software was adopted by the BBC, Disney, WorldCom, and Dell, along with other major international players. It was this single product that made NeXT such a desirable acquisition target for Apple in 1996.

While at NeXT, Jobs experimented with original management strategies. He wanted to create a completely new corporate culture and improve the sense of community. Jobs emphasized that his staff were not employees but rather members of the company, and as such they were entitled to many benefits. Until the 1990s, only two basic salary plans were offered—$75,000 to those who joined before 1986, and $50,000 to those who joined after.

Performance reviews took place every six months, and if you did well, you would be offered a raise. Staff were paid monthly in advance (rather than biweekly in arrears, as was the custom in Silicon Valley), and the company's health insurance plan was made available to unmarried and same-sex partners as well as married couples. NeXT's offices, designed by architect I.M. Pei, were almost entirely open-plan: Only Jobs's office and the conference rooms were enclosed. This fostered a sense of oversight by and of your peers and encouraged staff to work harder.

 Build the right environment to inspire creativity and hard work.

Although Jobs dedicated much of his time and effort to NeXT, it was not his only commercial interest at the time. He bought the Graphics Group from Lucasfilm in 1986 for $10 million and renamed the company Pixar. Although Jobs had no artistic experience beyond taking a calligraphy course in college, he understood the technology behind computer graphics and believed he could take the company into a new phase in digital animation. Pixar's first film was 1995's *Toy Story,* and Jobs was the executive producer. Other box-office hits included *A Bug's Life* (1998), *Monsters, Inc.* (2001), *Finding Nemo* (2003), and *The Incredibles* (2004), and Pixar won the Academy Award for best animated feature seven times. Jobs was fast becoming a force to be reckoned with in the film world, in addition to the world of computers.

Pixar's films had been distributed through Disney, and in the run-up to this contract's expiration date, Jobs renegotiated the deal with Disney's chief executive, Michael Eisner. Despite Jobs's efforts, the renegotiation floundered, but Eisner was replaced by Bob Iger in late 2005, and the story took an unexpected twist. Iger offered to buy Pixar from Jobs and his partners for an all-stock transaction worth $7.4 billion. Jobs jumped at the opportunity and consequently became the largest single shareholder, owning 7 percent of Disney's shares. He also joined Disney's board of directors.

RETURN TO APPLE

Through the 1990s, under the successive leadership of Sculley (1983–1993), Michael Spindler (1993–1996), and Gil Amelio (1996–1997), Apple was struggling commercially, so much so that Amelio described the company as "a ship with a hole in the bottom, leaking water." The IBM PC was dominating the computer market with a comparable GUI; Apple's new product lines (including Centris, Quadra, and Performa) were poorly marketed and sold erratically; and in 1995 the company decided to license the Macintosh OS and ROMs to third-party manufacturers, shortsightedly removing the Mac's unique selling point.

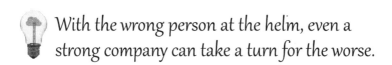 *With the wrong person at the helm, even a strong company can take a turn for the worse.*

What Apple's directors did do, however, was realize their shortcomings, in particular their need for a new operating system to take the company into the 21st century. NeXT and Be, Inc. competed against each other in the bid process, and NeXT emerged triumphant. Apple acquired NeXT for $419 million in cash, and Jobs personally received 1.5 million shares in Apple. He was invited back to the company, initially as a consultant, in December 1996 (when Amelio was ousted), and seven months later he was appointed interim CEO, a position that would be made permanent in 2000. Way back in 1985, in an interview with *Playboy*, Jobs had said, "I'll always stay connected with Apple. I hope that throughout my life I'll sort of have the thread of my life and the thread of Apple weave in and out of each other, like a tapestry. There may be a few years when I'm not there, but I'll always come back." He had foretold his own future.

> **"You can't connect the dots looking forward; you can only connect them looking backwards. So you have to trust that the dots will somehow connect in your future.... This approach has never let me down, and it has made all the difference in my life."**
>
> —STEVE JOBS

Jobs's return was a breath of fresh air into a company that had become increasingly stagnant in its ideas, projects, and personnel. Jobs terminated research-and-development projects he didn't feel had long-term viability (including Cyberdog, Newton, and OpenDoc); he identified a loophole in the Mac OS licensing contracts and used it to terminate them; and he shook up the company's management structure. Salon reported that after Jobs's return, Apple employees tried to avoid stepping into an elevator with him, "afraid that they might not have a job when the doors opened," but in reality only a few suffered this fate. Jobs did restructure Apple's board of directors, however, parachuting in some of the best executives from NeXT and allowing the two companies to merge.

Journalists were keen to report that Jobs had single-handedly saved Apple, but he didn't see it that way. When asked by *Businessweek* in May 1998 if his return would reinvigorate the company with a sense of magic, Jobs replied, "This is not a one-man show. What's reinvigorating this company is two things: One, there's a lot of really talented people in this company who listened to the world tell them they were losers for a couple of years, and some of them were on the verge of starting to believe it themselves. But they're not losers. What they didn't have was a good set of coaches, a good plan. A good senior management team. But they have that now."

Jobs's humility over this issue won him a great deal of respect among his Apple colleagues and the wider tech community. Apple's corporate recovery had begun, and Jobs was the man with both the vision and his hand on the rudder. Although he probably had only an inkling of it at the time, things for Apple were about to get very exciting indeed.

Using NeXT's WebObjects application, Jobs launched the online Apple Store in November 1997. WebObjects made the Apple Store quick to build—it took less than a year to design and make it operational—and in the first month of trading, the Apple Store generated $12 million in orders. This was the first time Apple had had a direct sales outlet: Until then it had sold products through third-party agents. The direct-sales model also enabled Jobs to implement his new manufacturing strategy, with products built to order.

Also known as "just in time," or JIT, this strategy was developed by Toyota in Japan in the 1950s as part of its philosophy of lean management, and it was something Jobs had tried out when building the offices for NeXT. When properly implemented, JIT enables a company to improve its return on investment by reducing its inventory and carrying costs. JIT requires precision and organization, but at Apple it proved very effective. The launch of the Apple Store was the first part of this process, and physical Apple Stores would open from 2001 onward, optimizing product visibility in the marketplace and ensuring that Apple, not an intermediary, would earn the lion's share of the profits on retail sales.

Although Apple and Microsoft have had a historic rivalry, Jobs took to the stage at the 1997 Macworld Expo to announce a five-year partnership. Microsoft agreed to release Microsoft

Office for use on the Macintosh platform and make a token investment of $150 million into Apple; in exchange, Apple settled a long-running dispute as to whether or not Microsoft Windows infringed Apple patents and announced that Microsoft's Internet Explorer would be the default web browser on Apple machines. Jobs was very much Apple's public mouthpiece, and people listened when he spoke. In reality, few people were interested in the minutiae of the partnership deal, but they did respond favorably to his overarching message: "We have to let go of this notion that for Apple to win, Microsoft has to lose. We have to embrace a notion that for Apple to win, Apple has to do a really good job. And if others are going to help us, that's great, because we need all the help we can get, and if we screw up and we don't do a good job, it's not somebody else's fault. It's our fault."

 Find an enemy! Great rivalries are the best advertisement.

The i Era

With the wind in his sales, so to speak, and Microsoft's highly regarded reputation as an added boost, Jobs strode confidently into 1998 and the start of an extraordinary period of innovation for Apple. The company would transform the world of consumer electronics with the launch of the iMac, the iBook, the iPod, and, of course, Mac OS. Yet again, Jobs emphasized the importance of aesthetics in the iMac's design process. The *i*, imaginatively, stood for "internet," "individuality," and "innovation," and was the brainchild of Ken Segall, an employee at a Los Angeles advertising agency. Jobs had originally wanted to call the new machine the MacMan, but he recognized the superiority of Segall's suggestion. The iMac's greatest selling point was its simplicity: Users wanted out-of-the-box experiences, and that's exactly what Jobs gave them, even when it was hard to deliver.

This wasn't just rhetoric. Jobs practiced what he preached. In one famous TV commercial, a seven-year-old and his dog were challenged to set up an iMac, racing against a Stanford University MBA student with an HP Pavilion 8250. The kid and the dog were ready to go after just eight minutes and 15 seconds; the MBA student was left in the dust.

 ## Don't sell products. Sell dreams.

Even more revolutionary than the iMac was the iBook, the first consumer-oriented laptop. The first model, the iBook G3, was nicknamed "the clamshell," and Jobs unveiled it during his keynote speech at the Macworld Conference and Expo in New York in June 1999. It was available in various bright colors (setting it apart from its cream- or black-clad competitors), and it was the first mainstream computer designed and sold with integrated wireless networking (i.e., wireless LAN). USB, Ethernet, and modem ports all came standard, as did the optical drive. The shape of the machine, which included an integral handle, was attractive and functional in equal measure, and it was also durable and reliable. Consumers loved it, and the iBook sold like hotcakes. It was the first laptop to be bought en masse for schools.

Two significant Apple product launches went hand in hand in 2001: iTunes and the iPod. Napster had already made online music sales a reality, and it was inevitable that Apple would follow it into the marketplace. Selling music was not enough for Jobs, however; he knew people would not be satisfied sitting at home listening to music on their computers but rather would want to listen to tracks they had purchased while out and about, just as they could do with a Walkman or portable CD player.

Early examples of digital music players were available, but as Greg Joswiak, Apple's vice president of iPod product marketing, told *Newsweek,* "The products stank." Jobs knew Apple could do better.

As with the iMac, the strength of the iPod lay in its combination of aesthetics and function. Jobs pulled together a team of masters in their respective arts, including hardware engineers Jon Rubinstein, Tony Fadell, and Michael Dhuey. They took inspiration wherever they could find it: Rubinstein discovered and purchased the rights to the Toshiba disk drive; the wheel-based user interface was inspired by a Bang & Olufsen BeoCom 6000 telephone; and the shape came from a 1958 Braun T3 transistor radio. Jobs decided not to use Apple's in-house software but looked for outside ideas, settling on PortalPlayer's reference platform and an interface developed by Pixo, whose staff he supervised directly.

> **"You have to work hard to get your thinking clean to make it simple. But it's worth it in the end because once you get there, you can move mountains."**
>
> —Steve Jobs

Jobs had no qualms about taking ideas from other companies and using them in new ways. For him, such stealing didn't have negative connotations but was rather part of the creative process. He explained, "Picasso had a saying: Good artists copy, great artists steal. And we have always been shameless about stealing great ideas, and I think part of what made the Macintosh great was that the people working on it were musicians and poets and artists and zoologists and historians who also happened to be the best computer scientists in the world."

The first iPod was Mac compatible, had a 5GB hard drive, and could store around 1,000 songs. Its launch marked Apple's branching-out point from computers to consumer electronics.

Jobs was a visionary and knew in his heart that the future of these fields was not in desktop machines but in multifunction, portable devices and the computer programs to run on them. This shift in focus was made explicit in Apple's name change from Apple Computers, Inc. to Apple, Inc., which Jobs announced during his keynote address at the January 2007 Macworld Expo.

The miniature components for the iPod led the way for the iPhone and iPad, the revolutionary iPhone being, in essence, a wide-screen iPod with the world's first mobile video voice-mail service and a fully functional version of Safari, Apple's web browser. It was released in July 2007 and took the mobile telecommunications market by storm, knocking market leaders Blackberry and Nokia into the past almost overnight.

The iPad, launched in January 2010, filled the market gap between the iPhone and iMac, and though commentators initially feared the iPad would take interest away from these other products, no such thing happened. Consumers bought into the brand identity and wanted to own all three items. What's more, Jobs's obsession with his products' appearance meant that, for the first time, electronics were cool. New iPhone models were released on a 12-month cycle, and committed fans had to have the new version immediately, every time it was released. New software functions such as Photobooth and FaceTime, and hardware features such as front- and rear-facing cameras, made every new Apple product irresistible. Apple shot ahead of its competitors, including long-term rival Microsoft.

 Turn consumers into evangelists, not just customers.

Jobs was hugely successful and professionally admired by his peers and employees alike, but he wasn't always popular.

He was a demanding perfectionist and always wanted to be one step ahead of the game.

This pursuit of perfection, not only for himself but everyone else, made it incredibly difficult for his colleagues at Apple to keep up with him. In 1993, Jobs made *Fortune* magazine's list of America's Toughest Bosses, and 14 years later the same magazine (which was, on the whole, supportive of Jobs and his endeavors), described him as "one of Silicon Valley's leading egomaniacs."

ILLNESS AND DEATH

In 2011, Apple had net sales of more than $108 billion and net profits of nearly $26 billion. The iPhone was outselling its nearest competitor, the Samsung Galaxy S II, by seven to one, and the company shifted more than 32 million iPad units that year alone, contributing more than a quarter of the company's revenue. Behind the scenes, however, all was not well: Jobs had been on medical leave since January, and in August 2011 he dropped the bombshell of his resignation as CEO on health grounds. He remained with the company as chairman of the board, but the markets shook with the shock. Apple's share price fell 5 percent in after-hours trading. For many people, Jobs's face and unique leadership style had become inseparable from Apple's commercial success.

The reality was that Jobs had been sick for a long time. He had first been diagnosed with a cancerous tumor in his pancreas back in 2003 and had announced the fact to Apple staff by mid-2004. Although the prognosis for pancreatic cancer is poor, and Jobs was suffering from a particularly rare form, an islet cell neuroendocrine tumor, he resisted medical intervention for the first nine months, attempting to combat the disease through changes to his diet. His reality-distortion field, which had proved so effective when creating consumer products, was not enough to overturn the medical reality. Harvard researcher Ramzi Amri, writing later in the *Daily Mail,* suggested that this delay in seeking conventional treatment had reduced Jobs's long-term survival chances to next to none. Jobs later regretted the decision, as he confided to his biographer, Walter Isaacson.

He had tried following a vegan diet, acupuncture, herbal remedies, juice fasts, and bowel cleansings, and he even consulted a psychic. None of these alternative approaches worked, and he underwent his first surgery in July 2004. The pancreaticoduodenectomy, also known as the Whipple procedure, appeared to successfully remove the tumor.

 Live your life to the full, personally and professionally, because no one ever knows how long they have on earth.

Jobs was not afraid to speak out about illness and death, though he understandably preferred to discuss them as though they were one step removed from himself. In the 2005 commencement address he'd given at Stanford University, he summed up his views: "No one wants to die. Even people who want to go to heaven don't want to die to get there. And yet death is the destination we all share. No one has ever escaped it. And that is as it should be, because Death is very likely the single best invention of Life. It is Life's change agent. It clears out the old to make way for the new. Right now the new is you, but someday not too long from now, you will gradually become the old and be cleared away. Sorry to be so dramatic, but it is quite true."

Your time is limited, so don't waste it living someone else's life. Don't be trapped by dogma—which is living with the results of other people's thinking. Don't let the noise of others' opinions drown out your inner voice. And most important, have the courage to follow your heart and intuition. They somehow already know what you truly want to become. Everything else is secondary.

> "We don't get a chance to do that many things, and every one should be really excellent. Because this is our life. Life is brief, and then you die, you know? So it better be damn good. It better be worth it."
>
> —STEVE JOBS

Jobs's respite from cancer was brief: Journalists watching his keynote address at Apple's 2006 Worldwide Developers Conference described him as thin, gaunt, and listless, in stark contrast to his usual lively talks. The official Apple line was that Jobs was in good health, but rumors abounded, and shareholders started asking questions, saying they had a right to know. Bloomberg inadvertently published a 2,500-word obituary of Jobs in August 2008, to which Jobs responded, tongue in cheek, "Reports of my death are greatly exaggerated," a line he'd borrowed from Mark Twain. Jobs and his Apple colleagues tried to avoid answering questions about his health, declaring it a private matter for Jobs and his family, but at the start of 2009, when Jobs was too unwell to deliver the keynote address at the Macworld Conference and Expo, he had to come clean. He initially put his problems down to a hormone imbalance but then claimed he had "learned that my health-related issues are more complex than I originally thought." Jobs announced a six-month leave of absence, appointing Tim Cook as acting CEO, and underwent a liver transplant in April of that year. CNN reported his prognosis as "excellent."

After his transplant, Jobs returned to Apple and worked for 18 more months. He oversaw the launch of a wealth of innovative new products, from Mac OS X Snow Leopard and the Magic Trackpad, to iPads with Wi-Fi and 3G and new models of the

MacBook, iPhone, and Mac Mini. The buzz around new Apple products, though stimulating, was also exhausting, and again in January 2011 Jobs announced a leave of absence on medical grounds. He continued to make public appearances, including at the launches of the iPad 2 and iCloud, but his cancer had returned aggressively and was taking its toll.

Jobs stepped down as Apple's CEO on August 24, 2011, writing to the board of directors, "I have always said if there ever came a day when I could no longer meet my duties and expectations as Apple's CEO, I would be the first to let you know. Unfortunately, that day has come." He appointed Cook as his successor as CEO but continued as chairman of the board.

 Know when it is the right time to step down and let someone else take the reins.

Six weeks after Jobs stepped down, he lost consciousness and died the following day, surrounded by his wife, children, and sisters. He had suffered from complications relating to a relapse in his pancreatic cancer. Apple, Microsoft, and Disney all flew their flags at half mast as a mark of respect. For the next two weeks, Apple's corporate home page carried a portrait of Jobs, with the following statement: "Apple has lost a visionary and creative genius, and the world has lost an amazing human being. Those of us who have been fortunate enough to know and work with Steve have lost a dear friend and an inspiring mentor. Steve leaves behind a company that only he could have built, and his spirit will forever be the foundation of Apple."

Jobs was buried in Palo Alto in a nondenominational cemetery. His grave is unmarked, and his funeral was a private affair for family and close friends. Separate memorial services were held for invited guests (including Bono, Yo-Yo Ma, and Jobs's former girlfriend Joan Baez) at Stanford University and a few days later on the Apple campus for company staff. Many Apple Stores closed for the day so employees could attend.

Jobs's death was front-page news around the world. More than a million people left tributes. *Time* magazine and *Businessweek* published commemorative issues with Jobs on the cover. President Barack Obama, U.K. prime minister David Cameron, and Microsoft founder Bill Gates all spoke out about Jobs's contributions to society. He was characterized as the Henry Ford or Thomas Edison of his time. In life, Jobs did have his detractors, but after his death these people were largely silent.

LEGACY

In the years leading up to his death, Jobs had collected every award and accolade imaginable: He was inducted into the California Hall of Fame by Governor Arnold Schwarzenegger in 2007; *Fortune* named him the most powerful person in business in 2007 and CEO of the decade in 2009; in 2010 *Forbes* ranked him at No. 17 on its list of the World's Most Powerful People; and he was the *Financial Times* person of the year for 2010.

The tributes didn't stop with his death, however. When in 2012 young adults were asked to name the greatest innovator of all time, Jobs ranked second, behind Edison, and he was posthumously given a Grammy Trustees Award for his services to the music industry.

What, though, was Jobs's legacy to the world? First, Jobs made technology cool in a way it had never been before. He was not only the face of Apple but of Silicon Valley and the computer industry as a whole. The prevailing view prior to Jobs's return to Apple, in the words of Sculley, was that "high-tech could not be designed and sold as a consumer product." Jobs knew innovation demanded people who could dream up the things others believed were impossible and who were crazy enough to act on their ideas.

 Strive to be an inspiration for the next generation.

Jobs's vision of turning Apple into a consumer-products company was said to be a lunatic plan, and he was completely happy about that. It confirmed that he was one of the crazy people, the rebels he admired. His plan worked because Jobs understood better than his colleagues or his competitors what the future marketplace would look like and what the demands of consumers would be. He took the tech industry out of the hands of computer geeks and catapulted it into the mainstream.

Unlike Gates at Microsoft, Jobs was not widely known for his philanthropy: He refused to sign investor Warren Buffett's Giving Pledge, and when he returned to Apple in 1997, one of the first things he did was to terminate the company's corporate philanthropy programs. It's not that Jobs wasn't generous or didn't believe in charity; like so many other things, he just preferred to do it his way, and unlike many other billionaires, Jobs didn't want to shout about his good works, preferring that the media concentrate their attention on Apple.

One major initiative Jobs did support through Apple, however, was the Project (Red) program, which encourages companies to create red versions of their devices and give the profits to charity. Apple has been the single largest contributor to the project's global fund since its inception, and the money goes toward fighting AIDS, malaria, and tuberculosis.

Jobs's personal wealth, which was estimated at around $11 billion at the time of his death, has been held in the Steven P. Jobs

Trust, run by his widow, Laurene Powell Jobs. The transfer of wealth has made Powell the ninth richest woman in the world. She does not discuss how she spends the money, but she is known to have committed time and funding to the Emerson Collective, which makes grants and investments in education initiatives; College Track, which Powell founded in 1997 to put students from low-income families through college; the East Congo Initiative in Africa; and the Dream Act, proposed legislation that would provide legal status for immigrants who arrived in the U.S. as young children.

In 1993, Jobs gave an interview to *The Wall Street Journal* in which he said, "Being the richest man in the cemetery doesn't matter to me.... Going to bed at night saying we've done something wonderful...that's what matters to me." It seems Jobs got his wish after all.

CONCLUSION

Steve Jobs changed the world more than any other person in his generation. He was content to be an outsider and a rebel because it gave him the freedom to dream and to try things that more conventional individuals thought impossible. His meteoric rise from college dropout to revered multibillionaire and tech-sector revolutionary took 30 years and was far from smooth, but he had complete and unshakable faith in his own abilities and was adamant that innovative thinking and hard work would pay inestimable dividends in the long term. He was right.

In this chapter we have learned unique lessons from Jobs, his life, and his work. Although they do stand independently, and it is right to think about each of them in turn, there are also five important, overarching lessons that encompass many of the smaller points.

- ▶ Work with the best people in the business
- ▶ Always be a step ahead of the competition
- ▶ Believe passionately in what you do
- ▶ Getting something wrong doesn't mean you have failed
- ▶ Be the change you want to see in the world

If you want to develop the best products, you need the best people in every post. However great you are, you need to delegate responsibility to others and should ensure that appointments and promotions are given on the basis of expertise (even if gained in other industries), rather than just because someone has worked with you for a long time. Trust the people you appoint, even if they are critical of you, and invest time, money, and effort in your commercial relationships so that your staff are loyal and passionate ambassadors for you and your brand.

In business, there is no point in looking backward: You need to look to the future and anticipate customer needs and wants. Staying ahead requires a never-ending stream of new ideas. They won't always work out, but you will always have something fresh on the drawing board. Don't let your imagination be limited by present realities; research and development can take many years, and by the time you are ready to launch (especially if you are in the driver's seat of innovation), technology will more likely than not have caught up and be able to meet your requirements.

Passion and commitment sell products. If you don't believe 110 percent in what you are doing, find something else to do. To be a success, you will have to commit all your time, energy, and money to your projects. We all get only one life, so if the project doesn't thrill you to the core, don't waste your life pursuing it. Stop, look around for another idea, and chase after that one instead.

Everyone makes mistakes. The way they deal with those set-backs is what sets successful people apart. Jobs launched some duds. He got kicked out of his own company. He didn't let it get him down. He got back up and fought on, but—and this is very important—he did so without resentment. He looked critically at himself and what he had done wrong, and he learned important lessons for the future. When Jobs returned to Apple in 1997, he wasn't the same CEO he had been when he resigned years before. We all have to change, and we all have room to improve.

Saying you want to change the world is not enough. Your actions need to support your rhetoric. Jobs knew that to revolutionize the tech sector he needed not only to design and release revolutionary products but to set the bar higher for the entire industry. He branched out beyond computing, encouraging other sectors to prioritize innovation and quality, too. The ethos he created and espoused, of always striving to be and do the best and then break your own records, will continue at Apple and in Silicon Valley as a whole long after Jobs's death. Steve Jobs would say you shouldn't aim to be just an entrepreneur or inventor. You must be a revolutionary, too.

Arnold Schwarzenegger

INTRODUCTION

Everybody loves the story of an underdog, the poor immigrant who came from depressed postwar Europe and shot to fame in the land of opportunity, the United States of America. Although it might make us green with envy, we also admire a Renaissance man, someone who excels in a breadth of fields, rather than just one. These two things may explain, in part, why Arnold Schwarzenegger—world-famous bodybuilder, Hollywood movie star, governor of California, and high-profile environmental campaigner—holds such an enduring fascination for us.

In every phase of his life, in every business and profession he has entered, Schwarzenegger has excelled. He has obtained high office, won world titles, made hundreds of millions of dollars, and married into one of the most influential political families in America, the Kennedys. He counts among his closest friends billionaire investors and presidents, rock stars, sports stars, and film stars. When he writes a book, it's a best-seller. When he makes a film, it's a guaranteed blockbuster. What is Schwarzenegger's recipe for success, and how can we learn from him? Surely it can't just be luck.

Schwarzenegger is passionate, capable, and committed. His success was not a one-off event; it is an ongoing endeavor, and Schwarzenegger has been working hard to achieve his dreams since he was a kid.

CHILDHOOD AND FAMILY

Arnold Alois Schwarzenegger was born on July 30, 1947, in Thal, Austria. His father, Gustav Schwarzenegger, was a police chief and noncommissioned military officer. He served in the Austrian army in the 1930s, and during World War II he saw action with Panzergruppe 4 in Belgium, France, Poland, Russia, and Ukraine. Gustav was a member of the Nazi Party, having applied voluntarily in 1938, but despite detailed research in various European archives, no one has unearthed any links to war crimes or the SS on his part. His service record was, it would appear, completely clean.

Gustav married a war widow named Aurelia Jadrny just after the war, in October 1945. Their first son, Meinard, was born in 1946, and Arnold followed a year later. Postwar Austria was economically deprived and depressing, and though hardworking, the Schwarzeneggers were poor. They were a conservative Catholic family, and discipline was considered very important: Arnold recalls being beaten as a child for his misdemeanors, and his brother was certainly their father's favorite child. In a 2004 interview with *Fortune* magazine, Schwarzenegger said, "My hair was pulled. I was hit with belts. So was the kid next door. It was just the way it was. Many of the children I've seen were broken by their parents, which was the German-Austrian mentality. They didn't want to create an individual. It was all about conforming. I was one who did not conform, and whose will could not be broken."

Arnold Schwarzenegger was closer to his mother, though she was a disciplinarian and made sure her two sons sat through Mass every Sunday morning. His father was a keen sportsman and music lover, and he instilled in his children an appreciation of both physical fitness and the arts.

At school, Schwarzenegger was a mediocre student, but his teachers described him as "cheerful, good-humored and exuberant." He was a keen soccer player, and it was his soccer coach who first took him to a gym. Although his father wanted him to follow in his footsteps and become a police officer, and his mother had it in mind that her son would go to trade school, Schwarzenegger knew from the age of 14 that he wanted to be a bodybuilder. It offered the chance of a more glamorous life and an escape from Austria to the U.S., a land that seemed to be paved with gold.

 Progress in life depends on action. Learn from others and think about how to apply those lessons in your own life.

Meinard Schwarzenegger was killed in a drunk-driving accident in 1971, when Arnold was in his early 20s. Though the two brothers had never been close—their father's unfounded belief that Arnold was not his biological son had no doubt created the rift between them—Arnold felt a sense of responsibility toward his brother's fiancée and three-year-old son. In a later interview with his then girlfriend, Barbara Baker, she said Schwarzenegger never spoke of his brother's death, and when his father died a year later, he informed her about it completely without emotion. He did, however, pay for his nephew's education and later helped him to emigrate to the U.S.

MR. UNIVERSE

It was as a bodybuilder that Schwarzenegger first made a name for himself. In a few short years, he went from being a teenage nobody in Thal to an international sports star with money, fame, and a string of attractive women at his side.

Early Training

Schwarzenegger officially took up weight training at the age of 15, though there is some debate as to whether he was in fact

41

a little younger than this. His official website biography has claimed, "At 14, he started an intensive training program with Dan Farmer, studied psychology at 15 (to learn more about the power of mind over body) and at 17, officially started his competitive career."

It was at this time that Schwarzenegger met a former Mr. Austria, Kurt Marnul. Marnul inspired the teenager and invited him to train seriously at his gym in Graz. Schwarzenegger was unusually dedicated: He broke into the local gym on weekends so he could train even when it was closed, and he felt physically sick if he missed a workout. When he wasn't training, Schwarzenegger was in the cinema watching his bodybuilding idols—Reg Park, Steve Reeves, and Johnny Weissmuller—on the big screen. By night he dreamed of becoming a bodybuilder, and by day he worked every hour to make that dream a reality.

> **"Strength does not come from winning. Your struggles develop your strengths. When you go through hardships and decide not to surrender, that is strength."**
>
> —Arnold Schwarzenegger

As an Austrian citizen, Schwarzenegger was required to complete a year's military service upon reaching the age of 18. Although this was a physically active program and provided a great sense of camaraderie, the commitment interfered with his bodybuilding training, so Schwarzenegger found it unacceptable. He went AWOL from basic training in order to compete in the Junior Mr. Europe competition. As he put it, "Participating in the competition meant so much to me that I didn't carefully think through the consequences." When he returned to the army, he was punished with a week in a military prison. It was, as far as he was concerned, a small price to pay to achieve the next step in his plan.

Pursuing your dreams sometimes has unpleasant short-term consequences.

Winning competitions in continental Europe did earn Schwarzenegger the chance to compete at the Mr. Universe contest. This was his way out of Austria and out of poverty.

Mr. Universe

Schwarzenegger flew to London for the 1966 NABBA Mr. Universe competition, where he excelled because of his determination and training. He lacked the muscle definition of his older rival, Chester Yorton, however, and finished in second place. But Schwarzenegger did catch the eye of judge Charles "Wag" Bennett, who saw the young man's potential. Bennett invited the teenager to stay in his already crowded home above a gym in London's Forest Gate neighborhood, and he devised a training program that focused on improving his muscle definition and power in his legs. This would remedy the apparent weakness that had let him down against Yorton. While living in London, Schwarzenegger learned a few words of English, which would be essential in the competition world and in meeting his idol and later mentor, Reg Park.

 You will not achieve your dreams on your own.

Bennett's investment and Schwarzenegger's commitment paid off: In 1967 Schwarzenegger again entered the Mr. Universe competition, but this time he won. He was just 20 years old, the youngest-ever winner. He surprised the judges and the more experienced competitors, but it was a portent of things to come.

Schwarzenegger had dreamed of moving to the U.S. since he was 10 years old: The American Dream he had seen in the movies beckoned. In 1968, when the opportunity to travel there finally arose, he emigrated to Los Angeles, training under Joe Weider at Gold's Gym in Venice Beach, and he won the Mr. Universe title three more times.

Mr. Olympia

Schwarzenegger had always been clear that he wanted to be the greatest bodybuilder in the world, and that meant winning not only Mr. Universe, but also Mr. Olympia, a contest founded for former winners of Mr. Universe to continue competing and making money; it was a professional (rather than amateur) competition. Schwarzenegger's first attempt, in New York in 1969, was unsuccessful, but he went on to win the Mr. Olympia title seven times, scoring his first win at only 23 years old. Only one person has ever broken this record of wins.

 Set your ambitions sky-high, and don't settle for second best.

Bodybuilding observers assumed 1975 would be Schwarzenegger's last Mr. Olympia competition: He had won convincingly against Lou Ferrigno, a feat later detailed in the documentary film *Pumping Iron*. Schwarzenegger had a surprise up his sleeve, however. In 1980, as he was training for his movie role as Conan in *Conan the Barbarian*, the running, riding, and sword fighting he was doing convinced him he was in the best shape of his life, so he decided he wanted to win Mr. Olympia one last time. Hired to provide the television commentary for the competition when it was broadcast, he announced his intention to compete at the

11th hour and won with just seven weeks of preparation. He then officially retired from bodybuilding competitions, going out on an indisputable high.

 Sometimes opportunities arise when you are not expecting them.

Pumping Iron

In 1977, Robert Fiore and George Butler released *Pumping Iron*, a docudrama they had directed about the 1975 IFBB Mr. Universe and Mr. Olympia competitions. Filmed during the 100 days running up to the contests and during the competitions themselves, the film focused on Schwarzenegger and his primary competitor, Lou Ferrigno.

The 1975 competition was to be Schwarzenegger's last: He had been a professional bodybuilder for a decade and had won the Mr. Olympia competition five years running. The documentary compared the two men's training styles, personas, and attitudes, showing Schwarzenegger to be an aggressive extrovert who thrived on publicity and the attentions of beautiful women. There is a subtext of psychological warfare, an area in which Schwarzenegger is clearly in his element.

Pumping Iron ran into financial difficulties during the final stages of production, so was released two years late and only after Schwarzenegger had helped to raise the funds to complete it. The documentary was given a cinema release and proved unexpectedly popular; it brought the previously niche sport of bodybuilding to a national audience, resulting in a significant increase in gym usage. *Pumping Iron* was a commercial and critical success, and it was Schwarzenegger's first real taste of the silver screen. His on- and off-screen rival Ferrigno also used the documentary to kick-start

45

his own film career: He was cast in the title role of *The Incredible Hulk* and continued to play such roles for the next 30 years.

 Make use of the platforms given to you to catapult yourself onto greater things.

Writing

Schwarzenegger published his first book, *Arnold: The Education of a Bodybuilder,* in 1977. A commercial success, the book combined autobiography and a weight-training guide. Schwarzenegger clearly enjoyed the experience of writing and signed up for English courses at Santa Monica College in California, then graduated from the University of Wisconsin–Superior with a bachelor's degree in the international marketing of fitness and business administration.

His writing, in part, is what has kept Schwarzenegger's image at the forefront of the bodybuilding industry. For many years he wrote monthly columns for *Muscle & Fitness* and *Flex,* work that caused some conflict-of-interest accusations when he became governor of California; as a result, he relinquished his editorial role in 2005, but he renewed his editorial contracts in 2013.

 You don't have to pigeonhole yourself into any one field.

Schwarzenegger's autobiography *Total Recall* (a reference to one of his earlier films) was published in 2012. It is divided into three parts, focusing respectively on his bodybuilding, his film career, and his politics.

THE TERMINATOR

Using the international platform and celebrity he had gained as Mr. Universe and Mr. Olympia, Schwarzenegger took the opportunity to launch a Hollywood career. Directors immediately recognized his appeal to fans in the world of sport but also realized that his incredible physique would make him the ultimate action hero.

Working at first under the pseudonym Arnold Strong, Schwarzenegger made his first action film, *Hercules in New York*, in the early 1970s. Still relatively new to the U.S. and speaking little English, Schwarzenegger had such as strong Austrian accent that his lines had to be dubbed in postproduction to make them comprehensible to American audiences. The accent, his long and seemingly unpronounceable name, and his unique body type appeared to be stumbling blocks to a successful film career; Schwarzenegger was advised time and again to change them all, but he persisted.

 Turn your quirks to your advantage, and don't be put off by being different from those around you.

Schwarzenegger won a Golden Globe Award for his portrayal of the male lead in the film *Stay Hungry*; this raised his profile sufficiently that he was cast in the title role of *Conan the Barbarian* in 1982. With its adrenalin-fueled fight scenes and sorcery, the film was box-office gold, and Schwarzenegger had hit the big time. It was an era of filmmaking when heroes needed muscles and great physical presence. Schwarzenegger fit the bill perfectly.

Schwarzenegger would not go down in Hollywood history only as Conan, however, but as the Terminator, a cyborg assassin programmed to kill a woman whose yet-to-be-conceived son would one day save the world. A 1984 sci-fi thriller directed by James Cameron, *Terminator* was the first in a series in which Schwarzenegger's character was both a hero and a villain. Films from the Terminator franchise were released in 1984, 1991, and 2003, and Schwarzenegger had plenty of time to make other films in between.

He appeared in the lead role in some of the most famous action and fantasy films of the 1990s: *Total Recall* (1990), *True Lies* (1994), *Batman & Robin* (1997), and *End of Days* (1999). He also branched out into comedy, with films such as *Kindergarten Cop* (1990), *Junior* (1994), and *Jingle All the Way* (1996), widening his appeal to new audiences.

> **"The mind is incredible. Once you've gained mastery over it, channeling its powers positively for your purposes, you can do anything. I mean anything. The secret is to make your mind work for you—not against you."**
>
> —Arnold Schwarzenegger

After appearing in *Around the World in 80 Days* (2004), Schwarzenegger took a break from Hollywood to concentrate on a political career. It came as some surprise to his political rivals (and possibly to his allies, too) that he returned to the silver screen in 2010 with *The Expendables,* the story of a team of mercenaries tasked with killing a military dictator and rogue CIA operative. A sequel, *The Expendables 2,* was released in 2012, again featuring Schwarzenegger, and he also found time in his schedule to shoot *The Last Stand* (2013), a Western action movie in which he portrays a sheriff fighting a dangerous drug cartel leader.

Schwarzenegger's films have grossed more than $3 billion at the box office. His heroic, high-profile roles made him a household name and brought him both wealth and strong connections to America's elite. Schwarzenegger capitalized on these significant assets to catapult himself into another, quite unexpected, period of his career.

> **"I just use my muscles as a conversation piece, like someone walking a cheetah down 42nd Street."**
>
> —ARNOLD SCHWARZENEGGER

THE GOVERNATOR

"The Governator" is Schwarzenegger's affectionate nickname, a compound created from his position as the Republican governor of California and the Terminator, his most famous screen role. His successful political career began in the early 2000s, and he went on to become one of the most influential figures in U.S. politics.

Political Affiliation

Schwarzenegger has long been a Republican, describing himself as fiscally conservative and socially moderate. When interviewed in 2002 about his political choices, he explained what he found when he arrived in the U.S., during the 1968 presidential election campaigns: "Everything [Hubert Humphrey] said about government involvement sounded to me more like Austrian socialism. Then when I heard Nixon talk about it, he said open up the borders, the consumers should be represented there ultimately, and strengthen the military and get the government off our backs. I said to myself, 'What is this guy's party affiliation?' I didn't know anything at that point. So I asked my friend, 'What is Nixon?' He's a Republican. And I said, 'I am a Republican.' That's how I became a Republican."

The President's Council on Physical Fitness and Sports

Schwarzenegger's first forays into the sphere of U.S. politics occurred in the early 1990s when he was asked to chair George H.W. Bush's President's Council on Physical Fitness and Sports. As chairman, he spent three years traveling to all 50 states, promoting fitness to schoolchildren and lobbying the states' governors to support fitness programs in schools. Schwarzenegger traveled in his own plane, at his own expense, and had a furious work ethic, often meeting with three governors in a single day. His chief of staff, a retired marine named George Otott, recalls, "When he walked in, it wasn't about the governor, it was about Arnold.... He has what we in the military call a command presence. He becomes the number-one attention-getter."

 Be the person in the room whom everyone else wants to talk to.

After President Clinton replaced Bush, Schwarzenegger took up a similar ambassadorial role as chairman for the California Governor's Council on Physical Fitness and Sports. In this capacity, he drafted and sponsored his first piece of legislation, Proposition 49: The After School Education and Safety Program Act of 2002, which made state grants available for after-school programs. He has also been active as a coach and international torchbearer for the Special Olympics, founded by his former mother-in-law, Eunice Kennedy Shriver.

The 2003 California Recall Election

For a number of years, Schwarzenegger had openly been considering running for political office and had discussed it widely with friends, advisers, and potential donors. His chance came with the 2003 California recall election. At the time, Schwarzenegger was on tour, heavily promoting his latest film, *Terminator 3*. His mind was never far from politics, however, as his answer in a July 2003 interview with *Esquire* magazine reveals: "Yes, I would love to be governor of California.... If the state needs me, and if there's no one I think is better, then I will run."

> **"Democracy is not a spectator sport. To keep it strong and to effect real change, you have to be involved."**
>
> —ARNOLD SCHWARZENEGGER

A petition to recall the existing governor, Democrat Gray Davis, qualified for the ballot that summer, and, ever the showman, Schwarzenegger gave a statement saying he would announce whether he was running or not during an episode of *The Tonight Show With Jay Leno*. The public and the press held their breath but generally leaned toward the view that he would not run, since his wife (a Kennedy and a Democrat) was against it. Not even Schwarzenegger was sure about what he was going to do until the day of the announcement:

He later confessed, "I told Maria I wasn't running. I told everyone I wasn't running. I wasn't running. I just thought, *This will freak everyone out. It'll be so funny. I'll announce that I am running.* I told Leno I was running. And two months later I was governor. All these people are asking me, 'What's your plan? Who's on your staff?' I didn't have a plan. I didn't have a staff. I wasn't running until I went on Jay Leno."

As he explained his reasoning to Leno, "The politicians are fiddling, fumbling, and failing. The man that is failing the people more than anyone is Gray Davis. He is failing them terribly, and this is why he needs to be recalled, and this is why I am going to run for governor of the state of California."

Schwarzenegger's political views were largely unknown, but he was certainly the best-known candidate. The national and international press picked up on his run immediately, and the news was full of predictions about the Governator. Schwarzenegger played to his audience, giving them memorable one-liners borrowed from his most famous films, including "I'll be back" at the end of his first press conference. The media loved it. He recruited to his campaign team actor Rob Lowe, billionaire Warren Buffett, and George Schulz, a former aide to Presidents Nixon and Reagan.

The recall election took place in October 2003. Governor Davis was removed from office, and 48.6 percent of voters chose Schwarzenegger to succeed him, giving him 1.3 million more votes than his nearest competitor.

GOVERNOR OF CALIFORNIA

Schwarzenegger faced a lineup of critics waiting for him to fail: With the exception of former president and California governor Ronald Reagan, when had a Hollywood movie star previously been successful in politics? But Schwarzenegger had a great deal of popular support—his approval rating hit 65 percent by May 2004—and was able to bring together politicians from both sides of the statehouse. He took a proactive approach to reform, repealing and introducing legislation from the start. Voters saw him as a man of action and, just as important, a man of his word.

Schwarzenegger's first responsibility upon entering office was to address California's pressing budgetary concerns. He developed and announced a three-point budget plan that involved floating $15 billion in bonds, passing a constitutional amendment to limit spending, and overhauling workers' compensation. Public support for the measures was at first lukewarm, but Schwarzenegger campaigned energetically and the requisite legislation passed. The International Bond Market reacted particularly well, uprating California's projections by three points, thus saving the state more than $20 billion in interest over the next decade.

> **"Political courage is not political suicide."**
>
> —ARNOLD SCHWARZENEGGER

Throughout Schwarzenegger's governorship, a number of issues emerged time and again, and Schwarzenegger's leadership has been a matter of much discussion. Among these, LGBT rights, the death penalty, and taxation have been the most talked about. As the Republican governor of a largely left-leaning state, Schwarzenegger could have found himself in a difficult position regarding LGBT rights, but he made the law, not personal or party views, the deciding factor in his campaigning and legislation. When in 2004, for example, San Francisco mayor Gavin Newsom ordered changes in certification to allow same-sex marriages, Schwarzenegger blocked the move—not because he opposed same-sex relationships but because the act was beyond the powers of the mayor.

Reinforcing this position, he went on the same year to issue Executive Order S-6-04 ("All state agencies, departments, boards, and commissions shall recruit, appoint, train, evaluate and promote state personnel on the basis of merit and fitness, without regard to age, race, ethnicity, color, ancestry, national origin, gender, marital status, sexual orientation, religion, disability or other non-job-related factors."); sign into law the California

Insurance Equality Act, which makes health-insurance providers offer coverage to employees' registered domestic partners, regardless of their sex; approve the Omnibus Labor & Employment Non-Discrimination Bill, which unified all state antidiscrimination codes; and sign SB 1193, the law that entitles the surviving spouse or designated beneficiary—including same-sex partners—of a deceased serviceman or -woman to a $10,000 death benefit.

 A strong leader is able to balance ideology and pragmatism.

The issue of the death penalty in California was more problematic for Schwarzenegger. As governor, he had the right to grant clemency to convicted felons on death row, though doing so is in itself a controversial act. Though Schwarzenegger granted clemency on a number of occasions and saved prisoners from execution, sometimes he chose not to: He denied a pardon to convicted murderers Kevin Cooper and Stanley "Tookie" Williams, for example, and both men were executed.

Schwarzenegger's economic and fiscal policies also occasionally brought him into conflict with the California legislature. Though in 2004 the Cato Institute, a Libertarian policy-research foundation, rated him No. 1 among American governors for his taxation and spending policies, Schwarzenegger often found it difficult to get budgets approved by the state legislature. When deadlock occurred, he many times spoke critically of his opponents, comparing them to children in kindergarten.

Schwarzenegger won his second term as governor in 2005. It was the most expensive election in California history—the total spending for both sides exceeded $300 million—and it didn't go well for Schwarzenegger: He lost all four of the reform initiatives he had proposed at the ballot, and he no longer had the political leverage he had enjoyed during his first term, which forced him to move toward the center in order to get legislation through.

In his second term as governor, Schwarzenegger focused on attracting investment into California to improve the state's finances and the perceived standard of living of voters. In defiance of President George W. Bush's moratorium on funding for stem-cell research, he allocated a further $150 million in funding, stimulating a nascent industry in California. He formed the Climate Action Board and worked with Democrats to agree to the Global Warming Solutions Act of 2006 (both actions in line with his role as an environmental campaigner), and he agreed to increase the minimum wage in California to $8.50 per hour. Such acts angered conservative Republicans but were popular with mainstream and left-leaning voters.

The global economic crisis, beginning in 2008, hit California hard, and with a state debt of $42 billion, Schwarzenegger struggled to fulfill his spending commitments. He suggested Proposition 1A to increase tax revenues to $16 billion, moved to replenish the California General Fund, and declared furloughs for two Fridays a month, on which state employees could not come to work and were not paid.

Schwarzenegger's second term as governor ended in January 2011, and he was not eligible for reelection. He has, however, continued to have an active role in politics and debate. Schwarzenegger wasn't the most obvious choice to front clean-energy and sustainability campaigns, but that is perhaps why he is so effective. Making use of his high-profile public position, his political influence and business ties, and possibly also the surprise factor that he is a Republican heavyweight using his voice to advocate for renewable energy, Schwarzenegger has become a key ally for environmentalists and reformers.

Typically mild-mannered and conservative, Schwarzenegger opened a 2015 Facebook post with the line "I don't give a fuck if we agree about climate change." By moving the debate away from the traditional front line between those who are concerned about the environmental and social impact of climate change and those who believe global warming is a hoax, he forced both sides to identify points they could agree on: how it is unacceptable that 7 million people each year die from fossil-fuel pollution; fossil fuels will not be the preferred energy sources of the future, because they will run out; and given the choice between being stuck in a sealed room with an electric car and a diesel- or gasoline-fueled car belching deadly fumes, we would all opt for the former. These aren't politically charged points—they're practical ones. Schwarzenegger advocates, in his own words, for "a smarter, cleaner, healthier, more profitable energy future."

In 2010 Schwarzenegger founded R20 Regions of Climate Action, a nonprofit organization that promotes and implements projects to produce economic and environmental benefits by reducing energy consumption and greenhouse gas emissions to improve public health and create new green jobs to strengthen local economies. Working in cooperation with the United Nations, R20 issues reports, brings regional governments together, and implements projects as diverse as LED street lighting in Brazil, waste management in Algeria, and solar-powered bakeries in Burundi.

In his personal life, Schwarzenegger appears to practice, at least in part, what he preaches. He adapted his two Hummer vehicles to run on hydrogen and biofuels, and he installed solar panels to heat his house.

President Schwarzenegger?

In her unauthorized biography of Schwarzenegger, journalist Wendy Leigh quotes him as saying, "I wanted to be part of the small percentage of people who were leaders, not the large mass of followers. I think it is because I saw leaders use 100 percent of their potential—I was always fascinated by people in control of other people." Having married into a political family (his mother-in-law, Eunice Kennedy Shriver, was the sister of President John F. Kennedy), perhaps it is natural that Schwarzenegger should have the highest levels of political ambition. But could an Austrian bodybuilder and film star actually become president of the United States of America?

At first glance, the answer is no: Currently only those born in the U.S. are eligible to run for the presidency, as outlined in the Constitution. Although *The Simpsons Movie* (2007) does show Schwarzenegger as president, it is just a fantasy. A constitutional amendment would have to be passed (as happens in the 1993 Sylvester Stallone film Demolition Man) for Schwarzenegger to be eligible for the top job. He has reportedly been lobbying legislators about a possible change, and if he were to file a legal challenge to the provision, some commentators believe the lawsuit could ultimately win him the right to run.

In any case, Schwarzenegger's support is considered highly valuable to candidates in Republican primaries. He was close friends with both former New York mayor Rudy Giuliani and Arizona senator John McCain, two main Republican contenders in the run-up to the 2008 presidential election, and remained publicly neutral until Giuliani dropped out of the race. McCain and Schwarzenegger shared similar concerns about the U.S. economy and the environment.

BUSINESS INTERESTS

Schwarzenegger made his first million before he was 30 and before he hit it big in Hollywood. He is a serial entrepreneur, forward-looking, organized, and an exceptional marketer.

His first business was in brick building. He set up a company with fellow bodybuilder Franco Colombo, and the combination of effective marketing and timing (the company was launched just before the 1971 San Fernando earthquake increased demand in the construction industry) brought them quickly into profitability. They invested the money they had earned in a mail-order business selling fitness products and training videotapes.

 No kind of business is too simple or too humble. There is money to be made everywhere.

Schwarzenegger used his money from the mail-order business, plus his bodybuilding-competition winnings, to buy his first apartment building. It cost him $10,000 and gave him a taste for real estate investment. Along with fellow celebrity investors Bruce Willis, Demi Moore, and Sylvester Stallone, he put money into the Planet Hollywood restaurant chain (a competitor to Hard Rock Cafe) and into shopping malls and residential developments. He took guidance from a raft of successful investors, including Donald Trump, Warren Buffett, and Milton Friedman, and used his contacts to make inroads into the film, publishing, and sports industries. He went on to replace Trump as host of the popular TV show *Celebrity Apprentice*.

PHILANTHROPY AND OUTREACH

"Stop the Madness"

Schwarzenegger made use of his public profile as early as the mid-1980s to campaign on issues important to him. One early

such project was "Stop the Madness," an antidrug music video endorsed by President Ronald Reagan and featuring a number of celebrities of the day, including Whitney Houston, David Hasselhoff, and La Toya Jackson. The video was broadcast for a six-month period in 1985 and 1986, and it sparked antidrug campaigns in Europe, as well as being adopted for public-service announcements in the U.S.

The USC Schwarzenegger Institute

Though Schwarzenegger is proud to call himself a Republican and represent that party in elections, he doesn't toe the party line to the detriment of common sense. Indeed, Schwarzenegger is intelligent enough to realize that some challenges we face cannot be surmounted by partisan groups, and a long-term, coordinated effort from multiple parties is required. For this reason, he has founded, and dedicates significant time to, the Schwarzenegger Institute for State and Global Policy at the University of Southern California, which was instituted to advance post-partisanship. It encourages political and business leaders, regardless of their political ideologies or affiliations, to work together to find the best solutions to benefit the wider population. A think tank and lobbying organization of sorts, the institute draws upon the work of academics, entrepreneurs, business leaders, and scientists and seeks to influence public policy and debate.

Schwarzenegger has laid down four guiding principles for the institute:

- Science and evidence have an important role to play in finding solutions
- Local solutions are often the best means to solve global problems
- Great innovation and great solutions rarely come from government but rather from individuals, entrepreneurs, and the community

• Future leaders, including students and young people, must help shape the solutions for our future

Clean energy and the environment are key areas of the institute's work, but education, fiscal and economic policy, health and wellness, and political reform are also of significant interest.

After-School All-Stars

The mission of the After-School All-Stars program is to provide comprehensive after-school programs that keep schoolchildren safe and help them to succeed not only in the school environment but also in life. Participants are taught life skills to keep them safe and healthy, graduate from high school and go on to college, have fulfilling careers, and be able to give something back to their communities.

ASA serves more than 72,000 at-risk youth from low-income families. The vast majority of these students are African American, Hispanic, or other ethnic minorities, and 85 percent of them qualify for free school lunches. Schwarzenegger sees the program, in particular its use of sports, as a way to give these students a sense of purpose and value, teach them discipline and teamwork, and instill in them aspirations.

WEALTH, AWARDS, AND ACCOLADES

Schwarzenegger's exact wealth is unknown. Conservative estimates range from $100 million to $200 million, though his 2006 tax return has been used to produce an estimate as high as $800 million. The breadth of his investments and the instability of international real estate prices make an accurate figure hard to calculate. What we do know, however, is that Schwarzenegger doesn't have to clip coupons: He spent $38 million on a Gulfstream jet in 1997 and took no salary while governor of California because he was making more than enough elsewhere. Having more money in the bank doesn't make him happier, as a 2003 interview in *The Guardian* revealed: "Money doesn't make you happy. I now have $50 million, but I was just as happy when I had $48 million."

The awards and accolades given to Schwarzenegger are, as one might expect, as varied as his interests and experiences. In addition to his 1977 Golden Globe Award for *Stay Hungry*, he has a star on the Hollywood Walk of Fame. The WWF declared him its Heavyweight Box Office Champion in 1999, and the WWE inducted Schwarzenegger into its hall of fame in 2015. The Schwarzenegger Institute for State and Global Policy, the Arnold Sport Festival and Arnold's Classic bodybuilding competition, and the Arnold's Run ski trail at Sun Valley are all named in his honor, and on the occasion of his 60th birthday, the mayor of his Austrian hometown declared it "A Day for Arnold."

CONTROVERSIES AND CHALLENGES

Citizenship

Schwarzenegger received U.S. citizenship in September 1983, and normally this would have annulled his prior citizenship, as Austria does not permit dual holding. Schwarzenegger requested special permission, however, and was allowed to become a dual national. But his subsequent actions as governor of California have caused some controversy back home.

Austria does not permit the death penalty, having outlawed the punishment in 1968. An additional piece of legislation, Article 33 of the Austrian Citizenship Act, states, "A citizen who is in the public service of a foreign country shall be deprived of his citizenship if he heavily damages the reputation or the interests of the Austrian Republic." As Schwarzenegger has not always used his right as governor to grant clemency to prisoners on death row, Austrian MP Peter Pilz demanded that Schwarzenegger's Austrian citizenship be revoked. His support for the death penalty contravenes Protocol 13 of the European Convention of Human Rights and, Pilz argued, therefore damages the reputation of Austria. To date, the Austrian government has ignored Pilz's demands.

Conflicts of Interest

As a high-profile public figure with diverse business and personal interests, Schwarzenegger unsurprisingly has often been accused of having a conflict of interest. These allegations have been made in regard to his finances but also assert that by spreading his time and energy too widely, he could not possibly give his job as governor of California his full attention. The first major such accusations were made in summer 2005, when the press reported that Schwarzenegger continued to hold a position of executive editor for two American Media magazines. He had had a long association with the publications and continued to write regular bodybuilding columns. He announced that his salary from the work—$250,000 a year—would be donated to charity.

More such arrangements came to light, however. The *Los Angeles Times* reported that he had a consulting contract that would earn him $8 million over five years, while *The New York Times* revealed another arrangement, with Weider Publications, worth in excess of $1 million a year, plus phantom equity. Though not illegal, such relationships called into question Schwarzenegger's votes on policies regarding the advertising and sale of performance-enhancing dietary supplements, whose makers advertised in American Media publications. In 2005 *The Washington Post* reported that American Media had paid actress Gigi Goyette $20,000 not to discuss her affair with Schwarzenegger.

Gropegate

During his first campaign for governor, a number of allegations of sexual and personal misconduct were levied against Schwarzenegger. Though he admitted to having "behaved badly sometimes" and apologized to those involved, the accusations lingered. The first date back to 1977, when Schwarzenegger gave an interview to *Oui* magazine. He discussed his sexual orgies and smoking cannabis, which he is also seen doing after winning Mr. Olympia in *Pumping Iron.*

Six women alleged sexual assault and harassment, reports of which appeared in the *Los Angeles Times* in 2003. Three claimed Schwarzenegger had grabbed their breasts; hence the scandal was dubbed "Gropegate." The other women alleged Schwarzenegger had also touched them inappropriately. No prosecutions have been made, however, and the allegations do not seem to have had an adverse impact on Schwarzenegger's career trajectory or his standing with voters.

Steroid Use

For a professional bodybuilder, Schwarzenegger has been unusually candid about his use of performance-enhancing anabolic steroids during his competitive career. The drugs were not illegal at the time, and he has described them as "helpful to me in maintaining muscle size while on a strict diet in preparation for a contest. I did not use them for muscle growth but rather for muscle maintenance when cutting up."

Schwarzenegger has been rather more defensive when the topic is raised by others. In 1999, Dr. William Heepe predicted Schwarzenegger would suffer an early death, stating that there was a link between his steroid use and later heart problems. *The Globe* tabloid made similar assertions, and Schwarzenegger sued both for libel. Heepe was forced to pay $10,000 in damages by a German court, and the tabloid settled as well.

PERSONAL LIFE

Schwarzenegger's first love was Barbara Outland, an English teacher whom he met in 1968, shortly after arriving in the U.S. Initially the couple got on well and lived together, but they were very different people and not at all compatible. As Schwarzenegger summarized the problem, "Basically it came down to this: She was a well-balanced woman who wanted an ordinary, solid life, and I was not a well-balanced man and hated the very idea of ordinary life." Their relationship was passionate but turbulent. Though at first Outland found Schwarzenegger to be a joyful personality, totally charismatic, adventurous, and athletic, she later described him as "insufferable."

In 1977, Schwarzenegger attended a charity tennis match where he was introduced to Maria Shriver by their mutual friend newscaster Tom Brokaw. Although Schwarzenegger was in a relationship at the time with a Venice Beach hairdresser named Sue Moray, he was very much open to Shriver.

The couple married in April 1986 and had four children—Katherine, Christina, Patrick, and Christopher. Shriver worked throughout their marriage as a news anchor and was a popular first lady of California after Schwarzenegger took office. Shriver championed the role of women in public life, encouraged community service, and in 2005 launched the WE Connect Program to give support to economically struggling families.

In the mid 1990s, Schwarzenegger had an extramarital affair with a member of his household staff, Mildred Baena, and fathered a child. He managed to keep the affair and the child secret for 14 years, but he was forced to confess when Shriver discovered the truth and confronted him. She made a public statement that her husband's admission was "painful and heartbreaking," and she asked for privacy. Shriver filed for divorce in July 2011, citing irreconcilable differences. Custody of the two younger children was shared between Shriver and Schwarzenegger, who live near each other, as do Baena and her son.

CONCLUSION

The length of Schwarzenegger's career and the breadth of his activities is mind-boggling. In a bid to understand the essential qualities of the man and what has driven him to such lengths, it is best to distill his lessons down into three overarching points.

1. You need to have drive to succeed.

People do not become successful by accident: Making your goals a reality requires sustained effort, often over many years. Your state of mind—notably your focus, determination, and persistence—are integral factors in whether you will achieve your goals. Schwarzenegger knew from childhood that he wanted to achieve great things and that through discipline and hard work he could make them happen. He has never lost sight of the fact that even when lucky opportunities do come his way, he must still be the driving force behind his career if he wants to succeed.

2. Decide what you are going to do, and give it your all.

There is no point in making a half-hearted attempt at something. If it is worthwhile doing, it is worth doing properly. If you focus your attention and effort, and put in the hours, you will achieve far more. This applies whether you are developing a skill (bodybuilding, acting, learning a foreign language) or trying to gain experience, contacts, or a promotion at work. Nobody remembers the person who finished second in the competition or who lost the election. Give what you do 100 percent, and you stand a far greater chance of making it to No. 1.

3. Be open to opportunities and capitalize on them.

When Schwarzenegger became Mr. Universe, he could never have foreseen that one day he would be governor of California; he had never even been to the USA! What he did know, however, is that throughout your life, doors open to you, and they are not always the ones you expect. You have to keep your mind open to new ideas and possibilities and use your existing platforms, skills, contacts, and experiences to pursue them.

There is no doubt that Arnold Schwarzenegger has more achievements to come and more surprises up his sleeve or that he will continue to be a prominent figure in American politics, business, sports, and entertainment for many years. Although he has overcome a number of hurdles, and his personal and professional lives have not been without controversy, he remains a strong and, on the whole, positive role model for ambitious individuals in all walks of life.

Bill Gates

INTRODUCTION

Few leaders in the business world are as revered or renowned as Bill Gates. His name has become synonymous with innovation and leadership in the software industry, enormous success, and unheard-of wealth. Many look to Gates's story as an inspiration and a blueprint for pursuing their own entrepreneurial dreams.

It is unsurprising that the world's richest man is one from whom we have so much to learn. Thanks to the values instilled by his encouraging parents, the strengths of his own instinctive personality, and the people and events that influenced him at various stages of his life, the traits we will examine in this chapter—openness to risk, lateral thinking, a competitive spirit, strategic branding, keeping focus, overcoming adversity, maintaining adaptability, and displaying humility—all combined to drive Gates's incredible success.

EARLY YEARS

On October 28, 1955, William Henry Gates III was born into an upper-middle-class Seattle, Washington, family. Gates was the middle child, with one older sister, Kristi, and one younger sister, Libby. Gates's father, known as William H. Gates, Sr., was a prominent lawyer, while his mother, Mary Maxwell Gates, was a well-respected teacher and local business figure who held positions on a number of company boards throughout her long career. Bill's childhood was a happy and carefree one, and he enjoyed the healthy, active social life that many parents dream of for their children. He participated regularly in various sports, was a member of the Cub Scouts, and spent summers with his family surrounded by nature in Bremerton, Washington.

When Gates was 13, his parents enrolled him in the exclusive Seattle Lakeside School, which was the perfect environment to nurture his creative and competitive spirit. Before this move, Bill had experienced some difficulties with fitting in—he lacked direction and seemed to be having behavioral problems at the transition to becoming a teenager. At the age of 11, Gates developed rather rapidly intellectually and began to display a high level of emotional independence and rebelliousness. He bristled against the authority of his parents, particularly his mother's. When he was 12, his parents sent him for counseling to address some of these issues. Clearly a highly intelligent child, he needed the greater focus and discipline a school like Lakeside could provide. There, in 1968, he discovered his love for computers when the school fortuitously purchased a computer link terminal.

Although computers at the time were too prohibitively expensive for the school to own outright, the strategy allowed the school to lease computer time for its students via the link-up terminal on a machine owned by General Electric. Interestingly, Lakeside didn't permit its students to use the machine in a tightly controlled environment but rather allowed them a degree of relative freedom—an approach Gates holds responsible for his exploding teenage interest in computers. Also at Lakeside, Bill met his longtime friend and future business partner Paul Allen. During this time, the pair got their first taste of business collaboration, working together to create a traffic-counting program called Traf-O-Data. Although this particular scheme wasn't remarkably successful, it laid the foundation for future cooperation between the two young entrepreneurs.

Take advantage of every opportunity presented to you to discover and grow your passion.

After doing especially well on his SATs (achieving an almost perfect score of 1590), Gates was accepted to Harvard University. Although he was set on becoming a lawyer—a path his parents had actively encouraged from early on in his academic career—his true interests lay elsewhere. He was particularly gifted at mathematics, but upon discovering that he was not Harvard's best math student, he quickly lost interest in pursuing it as his major. Instead, he diverted a lot of his efforts into computer science. While at Harvard, he reconnected with his former schoolmate Paul Allen, who had dropped out of university in Washington and moved to Boston, Massachusetts, where he worked for tech conglomerate Honeywell as a programmer. United again, the pair eventually collaborated and conspired to form their own company: Microsoft. Following Allen's lead, Gates soon dropped out of college to pursue his business venture full-time. He moved to Albuquerque, New Mexico, and worked with Allen to establish the company there.

Gates later explained that the sense of urgency he and Allen felt to pursue their business dreams justified leaving college in his final year: "I loved college. It was so exciting to have conversations with lots of really smart people my age and to learn from great professors. But in December of 1974, when my friend Paul Allen showed me the issue of *Popular Electronics* that had the Altair 8800 on the cover, we knew it was the beginning of a major change [that] would make computers affordable for the average person someday.... We wanted to be among the first to start a business to write software for this new generation of computers. We were afraid if we waited, someone else would beat us to it.... And while I would never encourage anyone to drop out of school, for me, it turned out to be the right choice."

71

MICROSOFT AND BEYOND

The small start-up's big break came when IBM commissioned Microsoft to develop the software to be used on its machines. Gates and Allen arranged this by purchasing the rights to the third-party software that would form the basis of their soon-to-be-ubiquitous operating system MS-DOS, then selling the licenses to run it to IBM while retaining their ownership rights. In doing so, Microsoft not only profited from the initial deal with IBM but also earned royalty fees for each machine the software was installed on. When the personal-computing industry really took off, in the early to mid-1980s, Gates and Allen were able to offer the same licensing deal for the same software to IBM's competitors, as the company held no ownership rights or patents to the operating system they had originally commissioned. This business-minded stroke of genius was the deal that led to Gates's early fortune.

Gates became the sole representative of Microsoft when Allen fell ill with Hodgkin's disease in 1982. In 1985, Gates launched the first version of Microsoft Windows, which would become the almost universal basis on which personal computers would operate for at least the next 20 years. Microsoft went public on March 13, 1986, a move that was incredibly well received by investors. The initial public offering saw the company's stocks valued at $21 per share. While the sale of Microsoft shares at the IPO made Gates his first million (specifically, around $1.6 million), the 45 percent share of the company he retained made him the bulk of his fortune. By July 1986, Gates's share in Microsoft was worth around $350 million. In 1987, Gates became the world's youngest-ever billionaire, at the age of 31, and by 39, he was officially the world's richest man, with a total net wealth of $12.9 billion.

Gates continued at Microsoft as CEO, a position he held until he stepped down from it in 2000. He was replaced in this role by his Harvard friend and roommate Steve Ballmer, and Gates continued at the company in the position of chief software architect. In 2006, Gates announced he would step down as an executive at Microsoft in order to focus his efforts on philanthropy through his Bill & Melinda Gates Foundation. He transitioned from a full-time to a part-time role at Microsoft by 2008 but retained his position as a non-executive chairman at the company.

With the promotion of Satya Nadella to the chief executive position in 2014, Gates relinquished his post as Microsoft chairman for the title "founder and technology adviser." Gates's priority had clearly become philanthropy, on which he now spends at least two-thirds of his time. He has funneled a huge chunk of his personal fortune through the Gates Foundation, which is dedicated to fighting "extreme poverty and poor health in developing countries and the failures of America's education system." He is estimated to have donated around $28 billion to it. Through his work in this area, Gates is now known as not only the world's richest man but one of its most generous.

KEY TRAITS

Openness to Risk

As a young boy, Bill loved playing board games, and his favorite was the aptly named Risk. The objective of this popular game is to move your armies across a world map, attacking your competitors and defending your territories, in pursuit of world domination. The risk in the game comes in deciding where to attack and how to spread your armies through your territories. Of course, this risk is magnified because a battle's outcome is not necessarily decided by skill or strategy but by a roll of the dice. Much like the board game he loved as a child, Gates's life has been heavily guided by calculated risk, as well as the invisible hand of Lady Luck.

From an early age, Gates seemed aware of the need to take risks to enjoy rewards. Despite knowing that there could be severe consequences, he and his fellow computer enthusiasts at the Lakeside School researched and exploited bugs that would let them have more time on the school's computer link terminal. Although Gates and the other implicated students were consequently punished with restrictions on their computer usage that summer, this is clear evidence of an individual with an appetite for calculated risk.

Perhaps the first major personal risk Gates took was dropping out of Harvard to pursue his business aspirations. The Gates family had always revered education, and Bill's parents encouraged his natural curiosity from his early childhood. He was the kind of kid who asked a lot of questions, a trait his patient parents helped nurture by emphasizing the importance of reading and self-guided learning. Despite being great advocates of the public education system, Gates's parents sent him to private school because they wanted to provide him with an optimal learning environment for his personality.

There was little surprise, therefore, when Gates was accepted to Harvard—a seemingly predestined course thanks to his natural abilities and his parents' encouragement. So when Gates decided to take a leave of absence, it was a serious move. He knew his parents would be unhappy, and although they were taken aback by his choice, when they saw how much he wanted to pursue the dream of running his own company, they offered him their full support. According to Gates, he told his father at the time that he planned on returning to Harvard. It took 32 years, but Gates indeed went back, in 2007—when he received an honorary doctorate.

Much of the innovation required for a business to develop involves a good deal of risk, and this was certainly the case at

Microsoft. From the inception of the company, in 1975, through the mid-2000s, Gates directed much of the product conception and oversaw some significant projects, including the famous contract with IBM that led to the creation of MS-DOS and the launch of Microsoft Windows 95. Other projects were less successful, however, such as the poorly received Windows Vista and the company's early lackluster foray into the world of smartphone software. What's important to remember, though, is that had Gates not driven Microsoft to take risks with new products, it would be a relic of the technological past, much like the Commodore 64 gaming console or the floppy disk. Instead, thanks to the risks exemplified by Microsoft's changing focus in a dynamic tech world, the company has managed to stay incredibly relevant by today's standards and continues to innovate ahead of its competitors in some areas.

 Analyze the size of the risk and the potential for return—if either points to an unpalatable outcome, rethink your strategy.

Interestingly, some of the damage to Microsoft's reputation over time has resulted from the company's failure to take risks on certain concepts. A clear example is the development of internet browsing software and related technologies. In an infamous, perhaps apocryphal quote from 1993, Gates is rumored to have bluntly stated that Microsoft was "not interested" in the internet. Later, in 1998, he admitted, "Sometimes we do get taken by surprise. For example, when the internet came along, we had it as a fifth or sixth priority." This was arguably a valuable learning experience. By ignoring the initial buzz surrounding the internet and not taking risks to embrace the new medium, Microsoft paid dearly in the long run. It would be surprising to see Gates or the company make a similar mistake in the future.

Whether leaving school or taking chances on innovation, Gates was never reckless with the risks he took. There was always a clear goal in sight, limited exposure, and calculated risk. He could have easily returned to college, for example, had his business venture fallen through. Microsoft's endeavors were often hugely impactful but rarely radical. Although many of Gates's critics have claimed this simply displays a lack of creativity rather than careful risk management, it is a method that has proved incredibly successful.

Lateral Thinking

Lateral thinking, or thinking outside the box, has led to some of the most famous solutions to the greatest quandaries in history. For the average individual, lateral thinking can help us achieve solutions to problems in daily life, and it is often tested for in job interviews for competitive positions. When it comes to creative thinking, few people have practiced it as successfully in the business world as Gates. Perhaps his most famous demonstration occurred when he and Allen were commissioned by the computing-industry behemoth IBM to supply the operating system for its machines.

In the mid-1970s, Microsoft enjoyed some early success with Altair BASIC, the company's foundational product. This was the first high-level programming language available for the Altair 8800, a microcomputer that heralded the start of the personal-computing era. Altair BASIC was the first in a range of programming-language systems that came to be known as Microsoft BASIC, which became a common feature in personal computers from the late 1970s through the early 1980s. At the time, Microsoft's debut product enjoyed hundreds of thousands of users, and the success of Microsoft BASIC attracted the attention of many in the fledgling computer industry, including the world's biggest name in computing, IBM. In July 1980, after IBM's efforts to obtain an operating system from Digital Research, a more established company, failed, IBM solicited Gates and Allen to provide the proprietary software for its range of personal computers. The pair agreed to the deal, but they had one small problem—they didn't have an operating system to sell.

On July 27, 1981, Microsoft acquired QDOS (Quick and Dirty Operating System) from Seattle Computer Products for the tidy sum of $50,000. This would become the basis for MS-DOS (Microsoft Disk Operating System), which Microsoft modified according to IBM's specifications. Despite being more-than-competent software programmers, both Gates and Allen knew the real opportunity of their deal with IBM had nothing to do with creating an original, revolutionary piece of software.

> **"The finest pieces of software are those where one individual has a complete sense of exactly how the program works. To have that, you have to really love the program and concentrate on keeping it simple, to an incredible degree."**
>
> —BILL GATES

This would have taken years of development and testing and cost an enormous amount of money and time. Such a feat was beyond Microsoft's capabilities. IBM also needed fast results; having to wait years for a final product could have killed the deal. Though IBM was typically fastidious in its research and development, it had come to realize that PC design and rollout depended heavily on quick turnaround in order for the technology inside a machine to remain relevant. With this in mind, Gates and Allen saw the value of purchasing the rights to an off-the-shelf operating system that had already been thoroughly developed and tested for bugs and, after some minor tweaking, had all the makings of a functional piece of software. The real genius in the Microsoft–IBM deal, however, had nothing to do with the functionality of the operating system and everything to do with the concept of software ownership.

In negotiating to charge IBM a licensing fee for MS-DOS rather than selling the rights to it, Gates and Allen got a hold of the goose that laid the golden egg. Their arrangement ensured Microsoft was paid a royalty fee for each machine the operating system was installed on. Microsoft also wrote a non-exclusivity clause into its deal with IBM, allowing the company to sell the software directly to IBM's competitors. During the following decade, dozens of competitors sprang up, and almost all their machines ran MS-DOS. The decision to push for this deal displayed an incredible amount of foresight and lateral thinking. Many in the fledgling PC industry, including IBM, firmly believed the real business potential in the field lay in proprietary hardware. But Microsoft saw the moneymaking potential of software and, through the establishment of MS-DOS, was able to dominate the industry in this area and reap unprecedented financial rewards. This deal made fortunes for Gates and Allen and catapulted Microsoft into the spotlight as the single most important software company in existence.

 Those who can think laterally have a fundamental advantage because most people cannot.

Many of history's truly great minds have evidenced a high capability for lateral thinking, a talent that is particularly well received in the business world. And when we think in a truly unique way to find solutions to complex problems, we have a greater chance of enjoying gains based on our ability to *act* in a unique way.

Competitive Spirit

A spirit of competitiveness was actively fostered during Gates's childhood in a family that encouraged and rewarded healthy competition. Whatever game the Gates children were playing, "there was always a reward for winning, and there was always a penalty for losing," Gates has said. His parents encouraged his participation in sports and always rewarded his victories, however small. According to his mother, Gates was "competitive in cards with his sister, races to see who could do jigsaw puzzles faster, ski racing, sailing—whatever. He wanted to do it well, and as good as the other folks that he was with."

During summers Gates spent with his family in a rented cabin, his competitive spirit was again nurtured when his family and friends held their own "Olympic Games," and it developed further when he enrolled in Seattle's elite Lakeside School. According to Gates, "Lakeside had the kind of teachers who would come to me, even when I was getting straight A's, and say, 'When are you going to start applying yourself?' ... One day, [one] said, 'Bill, you're just coasting. Here are my ten favorite books; read these. Here's my college thesis; you should read it.' ... I never would have come to enjoy literature as much as I do if she hadn't pushed me."

At the helm of Microsoft, Gates was fiercely and famously competitive. He had a borderline obsession with being the best in the business and aimed to shut out any competitors. Microsoft's most famous rivalry was with fellow heavyweight Apple, and it carried over on a personal level between Gates and Apple cofounder Steve Jobs. The two companies' shared history is long and complex. They enjoyed a close relationship at first, when Microsoft worked to provide the productivity software that Apple's machines required to be competitive in the business world, but the rivalry really began in 1985, when Microsoft launched Windows, its first graphical user interface–based operating system (GUI), as opposed to the text-based MS-DOS. Prior to this, Apple had the only GUI computer on the market, the Macintosh. As Microsoft improved its Windows OS over time, it began to adopt more features that seemed to parallel Apple's system. In 1988, when Microsoft released Windows 2.0, Apple filed a copyright-infringement suit against Gates's company, which remained unresolved for many years.

Eventually, GUI-interface computing became the only way to complete many personal-computing tasks, which meant that it couldn't be copyrighted. Gates had also persuaded Apple to license the virtual displays found in its GUI operating system to Microsoft to develop Windows 1.0. In 1992, Apple's claim was dismissed, with the judge ruling that each of the above conditions nullified all of Apple's 189 contestations. In the long run, this ultimately meant Microsoft and other competitors could continue to use Apple's GUI-based platform as a model for the development of future operating systems. Microsoft and Apple had gone head-to-head, with the former coming out the clear winner.

 A competitive spirit can lead to innovation as well as success.

Although Gates may have won this fight against Apple, his desire to crush the competition landed him and his company in hot water in 1998, when the Department of Justice charged Microsoft with anti-competitive behavior. The company was accused of being a monopoly and engaging in abusive practices contrary to existing antitrust laws. These charges were filed over its handling of operating-system and web-browser sales, specifically Microsoft's apparent efforts to snuff out the internet browser Netscape Navigator by bundling its own flagship browser, Internet Explorer, as a free piece of software with the

Windows operating system. In 1999, a judge ruled that Microsoft was guilty of monopolistic behavior and had indeed made attempts to crush its competition. The judge ordered that Microsoft be broken up into two parts, one to produce the operating system while the other produced other software. Although this decision was overturned on appeal, the ordeal did a lot of damage to both Gates's image and that of his company. He came to be seen as an industry bully, and Microsoft was viewed as a selfish giant controlling the PC world.

 Do not let the spirit of competition become an all-consuming force that works against you.

Gates's experience with Microsoft has shown both good and bad sides of competition. His persistence resulted in one of his most successful pieces of software, Microsoft Windows, yet his dogged pursuit of the competition led his company to the brink of disaster. From this we can observe that there are indeed limits to the benefits of competitiveness. Fortunately for Gates, he learned his lesson from this experience without paying too high a price.

Strategic Branding

Paying close attention to branding is an indisputable key to success in business and everyday life, and Gates's experiences with it—in his personal branding and his company's—has shown just how essential it can be. Gates is a man with a healthy respect for the importance of good marketing; he once stated, "If you can't make it good, at least make it look good." Gates was closely involved with Microsoft's marketing from the company's inception. In the early days, he would spend hours planning and delivering the company's PR strategy. Initially, this involved spending a lot of time traveling long distances to pitch Microsoft products to potential buyers. Later Gates became the face of Microsoft and participated in a large number of interviews as the company began to enjoy success. He went on to appear personally in print advertisements for various Microsoft products and, at the height of the company's success, in high-budget television commercials.

 Public perception is one of the driving influences of popularity.

In 2008, Gates appeared alongside comedian Jerry Seinfeld in a series of Microsoft commercials, which were seen as a direct response to Apple's recent "anti-Microsoft" ads. Although the $300 million campaign received mixed reviews, it highlighted Gates's personal commitment to marketing. A more successful instance of his personally driven approach was the official launch of Windows 95. Long before Steve Jobs, in black turtleneck and Levi's, made Apple product launches must-see events, Gates poured huge resources into launching Microsoft's groundbreaking operating system with great fanfare. The company spent $300 million on the marketing campaign for Windows 95, roping in such celebrities as Jay Leno and the Rolling Stones to aid in its promotion. The system was a huge and unprecedented success, purchased by hundreds of millions of consumers and run on billions of terminals, and it brought in billions of dollars in revenue for Microsoft. The Windows 95 campaign was perhaps the first major example of making the previously unexciting concept of tech releases an entertainment spectacle of sorts. It set a model that many, including Jobs and Apple, would later emulate as a core part of their own companies' marketing strategies.

Despite his readiness to embrace and exploit the great marketing machine, Gates has also been on the negative end of public perception in a very personal way. Over time, he came to be viewed as the face of corporate greed and establishment wealth, which, as a figure who was named the world's richest man 12 years in a row, was a hard image to avoid. To make matters worse, Gates was not portrayed as the most humble of characters in several very public interactions. When called to testify as part of the *United States* v. *Microsoft Corporation* antitrust lawsuit, for example, he was perceived as very uncooperative throughout the process. He gave terse answers to most questions and displayed a lack of humility and a high degree of petulance, combativeness, and entitlement.

This was repeated when the European Commission ruled that Microsoft had violated its competitiveness standards and ordered the company to pay the single biggest fine in the history of the commission (the equivalent of $794 million). Though Gates and Microsoft were certainly entitled to object to the anti-competitiveness accusations they were charged with, the way this was done arguably harmed their image. Gates did appear to learn from this experience and began to take great pains to appear like a more relatable Everyman.

 Good branding involves not only deliberate marketing campaigns but also managing one's public image during unforeseen events.

In today's era of unprecedented attention to branding and public relations, we can all learn a valuable lesson from Gates's problems. While his efforts to coordinate and participate in Microsoft's PR campaigns were particularly enthusiastic, Gates experienced difficulties with the more impromptu moments that come with being a public figure under intense scrutiny. Somewhat cynically, some critics have even suggested Gates's engagement in philanthropy was part of an effort to redeem his and Microsoft's reputation following the anti-competitiveness lawsuit. That Microsoft began to decline in popularity shortly after the antitrust trials is perhaps no coincidence. In any event, Gates's ups and downs with image perception highlight just how important branding can be. Life is often a popularity contest, for individuals as well as corporations. Those who can present themselves and their interests in the best possible light can gain a competitive advantage by winning the support of their audience.

> **"If I were down to my last dollar, I'd spend it on PR."**
>
> —BILL GATES

Keeping Focus

One of the common misconceptions about being successful in the business world—or simply enjoying success in any venture—involves the role of good fortune. Many unsuccessful people believe others have succeeded because they have had more than their fair share of good luck. This toxic attitude breeds complacency and encourages laziness. Gates's story is often touted as a "right place, right time" success story, the kind where the stars aligned and the universe was in perfect harmony and just so happened to generate the kind of luck that made Gates a very wealthy man. While of course there was some element of luck in Gates's success, his dedication, hunger, and focus truly made his success possible. And though Gates came from a well-off upper-middle-class family, this was of no importance when it came to his motivation. According to his father, Gates had an appreciation for the value of money from an early age. Even after Microsoft became a roaring success, Gates would famously fly coach rather than first class when traveling for business to spare the company's travel budget.

Perhaps the best example of Gates's focus is in the attitude he demonstrated in continuing to improve Microsoft even after the company achieved monumental success. He displayed no urge to relax his fiery ambition, not even after earning his first million dollars or his first billion. Instead, Gates worked toward dynamic and shifting goals—for him, there is no finish line, only the next objective.

Gates's work ethic is famous and was instilled in him by his parents from childhood. In an interview, he once claimed, "I never took a day off in my 20s. Not one. And I'm still fanatical, but now I'm a little less fanatical." He was constantly working away at his prized project, building his company up to be the biggest and the best, and was simultaneously responsible for many different arms of the business in the early days, from research to business development to marketing. Whether developing new program ideas, negotiating business contracts, or traveling long distances to market the company to prospective clients, Gates showed his focus and ambition in multiple roles.

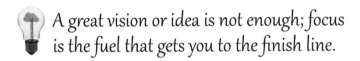

A great vision or idea is not enough; focus is the fuel that gets you to the finish line.

The hunger that drove Gates to become the world's most successful businessman is the same hunger that compels him to work toward solving some of the world's most complex problems. He appears to have brought the same level of intensity to this work that he did in developing Microsoft. He regularly travels to different regions of the world to raise awareness for global health issues and to oversee and implement programs sponsored by the Bill & Melinda Gates Foundation. He also campaigns tirelessly for causes the foundation targets, from vaccinations to poverty relief to education.

As one of the most obvious traits that can lead to success, focus is ironically also one of the most often overlooked. One of Gates's unique attributes is that his source of focus and hunger is seemingly inexhaustible. Success with MS-DOS was not enough, nor was Windows, and he has carried the same attitude to his work in philanthropy, from which many in the developing world may benefit immensely. Focus is a rather difficult trait to create out of nothing. However, it is most likely to be exhibited in pursuit of a goal for which you care deeply. If you feel you are lacking focus in pursuing your goals, it is perhaps time to reassess your objectives and question whether you are pursuing what truly matters to you.

> **"If I'd had some set idea of a finish line, don't you think I would have crossed it years ago?"**
>
> —Bill Gates

Overcoming Adversity

Though Gates's life has not exactly been peppered with tragedy, he has nonetheless had to deal with his share of adversity, which he had to overcome in order to enjoy his success. Indeed, Gates has also shown that adversity isn't simply something to be overcome; we can also use some of our more difficult experiences to help direct our future. This was a primary factor driving him to become one of the world's leading advocates for philanthropy and investment in solving the problems of the developing world.

Gates was particularly close to his mother, Mary. Of his parents, she was the most consistently involved with rearing him and his siblings. When she passed away in 1994, following a short battle with breast cancer, Gates was devastated. In a television interview, his father recounted an anecdote about his son being pulled over by traffic police while speeding to the hospital where his mother had died. But instead of wallowing in his grief at the sudden loss of his beloved mother, Gates made a positive out of his sadness by stepping up his work in philanthropy. His mother had taught her children about the importance of civic duty and the value of giving back. Mary Gates's emphasized this philanthropic spirit in a letter she gave to her daughter-in-law, Melinda, on the day of her wedding, a mere six months before Mary died. She reminded Melinda that "from those to whom much is given, much is expected." Following his mother's death, Gates donated $10 million to the University of Washington to establish a scholarship in her name as a tribute to her memory, her passion for education, and her spirit of philanthropy.

 Out of the darkness we can still find some hope.

Microsoft also faced a significant challenge when Gates's friend and business partner Paul Allen was diagnosed with Hodgkin's lymphoma in 1982. Though Allen received radiation treatments and completely recovered from the illness, the experience reportedly affected Gates deeply and lent him some extra perspective on life. His friend's diagnosis also seemed to focus Gates, making him even more determined to drive Microsoft's success to new heights.

Gates faced many challenges at the helm of Microsoft, particularly with regards to the anti-competitiveness cases that were brought before the company. In possibly the most trying experiences of his professional career, he navigated these hearings somewhat clumsily, but despite this, Gates soon recovered and urged his company along a new path with a corporate restructuring, refocusing much of his energy on his philanthropic work. It would certainly have been easy in such a situation to become bogged down, but Gates showed an ability to bounce back and take a new direction after his difficulties.

It is important to be able to deal with any adversity that might rear its head, whether that comes in the form of a personal loss or a professional challenge. Although we may endure setbacks in life, we can use these experiences to create positives and a new focus.

Maintaining Adaptability

From nearly the beginning, Microsoft was a giant in the world of personal computing. But one of the difficulties with early success is being able to sustain it over time. For Microsoft, this has been possible thanks to its adaptability, which has very often been driven by Gates himself. Perhaps some of his ability to adapt came from having been encouraged to participate in a broad range of activities as a child. During his time at the Lakeside School, Gates excelled in a wide array of subjects, including math, science, English, and drama. His parents emphasized the importance of a varied education, which was exemplified in their son's changes of career aspirations while at college, from law to math to computer programming.

Microsoft owes its most famous early success to its adaptability. Before being approached by IBM to provide the proprietary software for its machines, Microsoft had no experience in operating systems. It had created computer language programs such as Altair BASIC, but this was a vastly different exercise from creating PC operating-system software. When Microsoft began discussions with IBM, Gates referred the company to Digital Research, a firm that was already well established in the provision of operating systems, but when it became apparent that the company was unwilling to do business with IBM, Gates and Allen changed the direction of Microsoft and seized the opportunity to take up the contract Digital Research had rejected.

> **"We always overestimate the change that will occur in the next two years and underestimate the change that will occur in the next ten. Don't let yourself be lulled into inaction."**
>
> —BILL GATES

Microsoft has sometimes shown a tardiness in adapting to changes in the tech industry, however, and it has paid dearly on these occasions. Take, for example, its approach to internet technology. Gates and his company were slow to embrace this now omnipresent aspect of personal computing. When Microsoft decided to finally assimilate its services with internet-based software, it was already too late. While it was somewhat successful in shutting out its main early competitor, Netscape Navigator, by including Microsoft's Internet Explorer with every copy of Windows 95, it did not explore the internet's full capital potential. This complacent attitude allowed competitors such as Google to later step in and dominate the sector. Despite spending billions on its online arm with services such as Windows Live (which pales in comparison to the internet traffic of Google's services) and purchasing Yahoo! for the significant sum of $44 billion, Microsoft has had a rather underwhelming online presence.

Yet Microsoft has exhibited a good level of adaptability in the console-gaming market. Though it would have been entirely plausible for the company to rest on its laurels and restrict its success to the realm of personal computing, Microsoft's experience with the Xbox has been a resounding win. When the product was launched, in 2001, it was a bold incursion into a field then dominated by the Sony PlayStation. Since then, the Xbox came to hold its own, carving out a loyal following of gamers across several generations of consoles, in particular the uniquely inter-active Xbox Kinect. The Kinect smashed records for the volume and speed of sales of a consumer electronics item, moving 10 million units in just 60 days. Although this success came during the leadership of Steve Ballmer, Gates played an important role in guiding Microsoft's product-development strategy during this period.

 Stay agile to take advantage of opportunities as they present themselves.

Perhaps one of the best lessons we can learn from Gates regarding adaptability is that it's decidedly easier to adapt when things are on a smaller, less defined scale. This is one reason it was so easy for Microsoft to switch to producing operating systems early on. One of the challenges of running a large and established company, such as Microsoft became, is the burden of previous success. Of course, it's a little too easy to judge the mistakes of Gates and Microsoft with the benefit of hindsight. Gates may be the world's richest man, but all the money in the world can't buy an accurate crystal ball.

Displaying Humility

A truly great leader is usually marked by a healthy dose of humil-ity. This all too infrequently exhibited trait can be misinter-preted by some as a weakness, but true humility is a sign of both immense power and the consideration of that power. Early in his career, Gates was not exactly a person who could be described as humble. It was apparent that he had immense faith in his com-pany, his ideas, and his potential to succeed, and he did not shy away from showing it. Of course, given the then unprecedented level of achievement he attained, it is surprising that he was as grounded as he was. Yet despite his youthful brashness and self-confidence, Gates evolved into a much more balanced individual, an attribute often gained with age and life experience.

Although he could have continued at the helm of Microsoft unchallenged, Gates stepped down as CEO in 2000 and relinquished control of the company even further over the following decade to spend more time focusing on philanthropic work. One can only imagine how difficult this move must have been for him. Although some have questioned the extent to which Gates actually did relinquish control of Microsoft during the tenure of his successor, it is easy to empathize with the difficulty of giving up executive control of the company that had defined his life. While Gates's ability to hand over the reins was admirable in its display of groundedness and perspective, his consequent focus on philanthropy shows an even greater level of humility.

 A lack of humility can ultimately damage one's reputation.

Although tagged as the face of corporate greed for much of his career (particularly during the late 1990s and early 2000s), Gates has more than redeemed his reputation with his philanthropic work. The Bill & Melinda Gates Foundation was created in 2000 as a channel through which the couple could coordinate their giving. Today it is one of the world's largest private foundations, with an endowment of more than $42 billion as of November 2014. The foundation is "driven by the passions and interests of the Gates family," namely "alleviating poverty, hunger, and disease in the developing world and improving the state of America's education system."

91

In 2010, Gates joined longtime friend and fellow multibillionaire Warren Buffett to create the Giving Pledge, a drive that encourages other billionaires to commit to giving away at least half of their wealth. So far, Mark Zuckerberg, Paul Allen, Steve Case, and Larry Ellison are among those who have signed the pledge. Gates has donated a significant proportion of his fortune through the foundation and is incredibly active in championing the goals of the fund and working to raise awareness surrounding the issues it tackles.

This final lesson from Gates on humility is perhaps the one that has most shaped him into the man he is today. We can see from Gates's life how an apparent lack of humility can be a boon; perhaps enormous success and complete humility aren't truly compatible and Gates wouldn't have achieved what he did with Microsoft if he had been more self-effacing in the beginning. But eventually, it seems, true humility is something even the smartest individuals learn the benefit of with experience, and it can become one of the most truly rewarding traits in life.

INFLUENCES

It seems that a solid family life formed an excellent basis for Gates to become successful as an adult. Gates was very close to his mother, who instilled in him many of her core values and beliefs, including a dedication to philanthropy and a healthy respect for education. Gates's father has also been a profound influence and continues to work closely with his son in an advisory executive capacity at the Bill & Melinda Gates Foundation, which highlights the respect Gates has for his father and vice versa. Gates's wife, Melinda, is also high on the list of influential people in his life. On meeting his future wife, then a Microsoft employee, in 1986, he was quickly enamored with her forthrightness, intelligence, and independence. Shortly after they married, in 1994, she helped to spur their move into philanthropy and has continued to play a central role in driving this objective, now the most consuming element of their lives.

Outside of family, a few other key figures have influenced Gates's life significantly. Investor Warren Buffett, Gates's longtime friend and fellow multibillionaire, is counted highly among them. The two have rotated between the top spot for the world's richest man in recent years and have also shared a commitment to giving back much of their enormous wealth to help others. The pair first met in 1991 through a mutual connection, although both parties were initially apprehensive about the meeting. They eventually hit it off, however, and Gates soon discovered that he had found a valued mentor in Buffett. In setting up the Bill & Melinda Gates Foundation, Buffett proved instrumental in offering Gates guidance. On this, Bill noted, "We talked a lot about the idea that philanthropy could be just as impactful in its own way as software had been. It turns out that Warren's brilliant way of looking at the world is just as useful in attacking poverty and disease as it is in building a business. He's one of a kind."

CONCLUSION

Notwithstanding the key figures in his life, much of Gates's success has been self-directed. Consider how early in life Gates achieved the bulk of his success. Even as a child he displayed many of the inherent personality traits that formed the basis of his later success: his appetite for both risk and competition, his naturally brilliant intellect and inclination toward lateral thinking, and his impressive dedication and focus. However, we also know that Gates developed many qualities along the way that helped make him a more well-rounded individual who was able to carry his success forward. His adaptability to change, handling of adversity, and ability to act with humility all helped to make Gates a more nuanced individual with more to offer, and to gain from, the world. Many budding entrepreneurs have attempted to emulate his formula.

Gates's achievements have been some of the most remarkable of the past century. His and Allen's foresight in filling a gap in the market before that market even existed resulted in one of the fastest accumulations of personal wealth in history. Gates also helped drive a fundamental change in how we all live our lives: Though not directly behind the technology boom that began in the latter part of the 20th century, Microsoft and its enormous success helped the industry explode in terms of investment, innovation, and accessibility. Finally, Gates has done more than anyone before or since in his philanthropy. His commitment to spending a vast amount of his fortune in helping the world's most disadvantaged people overcome sickness and poverty is exemplary, as is his drive to encourage other mega-rich individuals to do the same. In this regard, much of his impact is yet to be felt and will no doubt affect the lives of just as many, if not more, people than he has so far.

Despite his enormous legacy, we know Gates is not infallible. He has made mistakes and bad decisions just like everyone else. And a person with exactly the same positive traits might well have failed in his or her entrepreneurial aspirations if not for the crucial element of luck. Though it is very unlikely that any one of us will scale the same great heights, we can take lessons from his achievements and apply them to the pursuit of our goals in the world of entrepreneurship and beyond, and we may still be richer for it—by understanding the factors that shaped the most extraordinary life of Bill Gates.

Elon Musk

INTRODUCTION

It wouldn't be much of a stretch to describe Elon Musk—one of the most imaginative entrepreneurs of the 21st century—as a living legend. He has been favorably compared to visionary American industrialists Henry Ford and John D. Rockefeller, and when Hollywood producer Jon Favreau was making the film *Iron Man,* he even sent his star, Robert Downey Jr., to spend some time with Musk in his SpaceX factory to get inspiration for his character.

But for Musk, at least, it is not all about him. The estimated $12.9 billion he has made in business is almost a sideshow: He historically has grown bored of talking about himself and wants to talk more about his work, his companies, and what they are doing to change the world. In order to understand his success (and, one hopes, be able to replicate it), you need to understand two things: *why* Musk is doing what he does and *how* he is able to do it. He thinks, and does things, differently from everyone else, and that's why studying his lessons is invaluable.

BACKGROUND AND EDUCATION

Born on June 28, 1971, Elon Musk is one of the youngest and most dynamic of the world's self-made billionaires. His father, born in South Africa, is of British and Pennsylvania Dutch origin, and his mother is Canadian. Musk himself was born in Pretoria, South Africa, as the eldest of three children. His siblings are a brother, fellow entrepreneur Kimbal, and a sister, Tosca. Their parents, Errol and Maye Musk, divorced in 1980, after which Elon lived mostly with his father.

In South Africa, Musk was privately educated, first at Waterkloof House Preparatory School in Pretoria. He was an academic child, always buried in a book, sometimes for up to 10 hours a day, according to his brother. He was addicted to science fiction but also heavyweight nonfiction books like the Encyclopaedia Britannica. Young Musk was bullied throughout his childhood, including on one particularly serious occasion when he was thrown down a flight of stairs and beaten unconscious.

As far as Musk was concerned, education was simply "downloading data and algorithms into your brain"; hence he found conventional classroom learning exceptionally slow and frustrating. Almost everything he did absorb came from his own reading, not the schoolroom.

 A conventional education isn't for everyone.

Musk got his first computer when he was nine years old. Its programming guide was supposed to take the user six months to complete, but Musk mastered it in three days. He developed a simple video game, Blastar, using the BASIC language, and the precocious teen sold his game to *PC and Office Technology* magazine for $500. You can still play the game online today.

 You are never too young to start being an entrepreneur.

After graduation, Musk decided not to stay in South Africa. He didn't relate well to the culture and felt his entrepreneurial skills would be far better deployed across the pond. So he emigrated to Canada, where his mother's nationality gave him citizenship rights. He enrolled at Queen's University in summer 1989, and after four years—the last two spent at the University of Pennsylvania—Musk graduated with a BS in physics and a BA in economics. Showing his entrepreneurial streak early, Musk and his fellow student Adeo Ressi (who went on to become the founder and CEO of TheFunded and the Founder Institute, as well as a board member of the Xprize Foundation) purchased a 10-bedroom frat house at the university and ran it as a nightclub.

 The relationships you establish in college may well be some of the most important you ever have.

From Pennsylvania, Musk moved across the country to California, accepting an offer into a Ph.D. program at Stanford University. The lure of neighboring Silicon Valley proved irresistible to the 24-year-old, however, and he lasted just two days in graduate school. Even as a student, Musk had a pressing question on his mind: What will most affect the future of humanity? The five answers he came up with—the internet, sustainable energy, space exploration, artificial intelligence, and reprogramming the human genetic code—would determine his future direction as an entrepreneur.

GETTING STARTED

Musk knew he had to get onto the internet bandwagon or forever be left behind. He marched uninvited into the lobby of the software company Netscape but was too nervous to talk to anyone or ask for a job, so he turned tail and walked back out. Starting his own business seemed less nerve-racking, and Musk decided to keep it in the family. He joined forces with his younger brother to create a software company called Zip2. The first $28,000 of start-up capital came from their father. Zip2 has been described as a "primitive combination of Yelp and Google Maps, far before anything like either of those existed." The Musks worked around the clock, sleeping in the office and showering at the local YMCA.

> **"Work like hell. I mean you just have to put in 80-to-100-hour weeks every week.... If other people are putting in 40-hour workweeks and you're putting in 100-hour workweeks, then even if you're doing the same thing, you know that you will achieve in four months what it takes them a year to achieve."**
>
> —Elon Musk

Zip2 developed, hosted, and maintained consumer websites for media companies and enabled those companies to target specific groups of online customers. Many companies couldn't see the appeal of the internet—what was wrong with a listing in the yellow pages?—but as recognition of the internet's potential increased, so too did the appeal of Zip2's offerings, and the software was purchased by more than 200 media clients, including *The New York Times* and the *Chicago Tribune.* Musk was client-facing and a strong salesman who gained the company new business relationships, but his own board had concerns about his management technique and blocked his bids to become CEO.

Compaq (now a division of HP) acquired Zip2 in 1999, just four years after its founding. Compaq paid $307 million in cash, plus a further $34 million in stock options, so overnight the Musk brothers became multimillionaires. Elon alone is thought to have made $22 million from the deal.

FINANCIAL SERVICES

Musk took $10 million of his Zip2 earnings and reinvested it straightaway into a venture called X.com, an online banking and email-payments company. Musk was confident that internet banking and money transfer was a business about to explode. He was right.

X.com wasn't the only start-up operating in this field, however: Confinity, trading as PayPal, had also recently been launched as a payment platform for handheld devices. The two companies were operating out of the same building, so recognizing that there was no point in going head-to-head if they could work together and dominate the market, they merged in 2000.

 You won't always be the only person to come up with a great idea.

The merger didn't go especially smoothly. There were a lot of big egos in the room, all of them successful internet entrepreneurs in their own right. While Musk was on a fund-raising trip/honeymoon with his first wife, his partners staged a coup and replaced Musk as CEO with Peter Thiel. Musk disagreed with the decision but had to accept it. At the same time, Musk wanted the joint company to continue trading as X.com, thinking the names Confinity and PayPal would quickly date. Customer surveys showed that the general public equated the name X.com with something that might be X-rated, which was a serious stumbling block for the brand. Musk was therefore forced to admit defeat and reverted to using the name PayPal in 2001. This was the right decision: PayPal was clear about what it did in a way that X.com was not.

PayPal grew rapidly on the back of a viral marketing campaign; new subscribers were automatically recruited when they received funds using the software. It was simple to use, free for buyers, affordable for sellers, and answered growing needs for better financial security online. The company went public in October 2002, and after it was acquired by eBay, Musk alone (as PayPal's largest shareholder) netted $165 million in eBay stock. The total value of PayPal at the time was $1.5 billion. Musk had been catapulted into the financial stratosphere.

SPACE: THE FINAL FRONTIER?

Before the ink was even dry on the sale of PayPal, Musk was already looking at his future options. He had always been fascinated by outer space and space technology, and he wanted to reinvigorate interest in space exploration and get increased funding for NASA, both of which had diminished since the end of the Cold War. His first idea was to create a Mars Oasis, a miniature greenhouse project on the red planet, where he could experiment with growing food crops.

 Sometimes even the sky isn't the limit.

Musk traveled to Russia with Jim Cantrell, an established fixer in the aerospace industry, and his old business partner from college, Adeo Ressi. The three men planned to buy refurbished Dnepr-1 rockets, converted intercontinental ballistic missiles that could be used to launch satellites into space. They met with some major Russian aerospace companies, but the Russians didn't take them seriously—they had no experience in satellites or other space technologies and seemed like wealthy time-wasters. Musk came home empty-handed.

They returned to Russia a year later, this time with Mike Griffin, formerly of NASA's Jet Propulsion Laboratory, who was now working with spacecraft and satellite manufacturer Orbital Sciences. He gave the group more professional credibility, and the Kosmotras company offered Musk one rocket for $8 million. Believing he was being cheated, Musk stormed out of the meeting. On the flight home, he calculated he could build his own rockets far more cost-effectively, estimating that the raw materials needed were only 3 percent of the total sales price of a rocket. Even enjoying a 70 percent gross margin, Musk reckoned he could cut the launch price by a factor of 10. Vertical integration and a modular approach would be key. The seeds of SpaceX were sown.

Musk's aim with SpaceX was to create a simple, inexpensive, reusable space rocket that would reduce the cost of space transportation and ultimately make the human colonization of Mars viable. Musk was determined to work with the best in the business, so he approached Tom Mueller, an employee of aerospace conglomerate TRW, Inc. and the inventor of the world's largest amateur liquid-fuel rocket engine. The pair founded SpaceX in El Segundo, California, and immediately got to work. Their first rocket, Falcon 1 (named in honor of *the* Millennium Falcon from Star Wars) was developed and manufactured between 2006 and 2009 and became the first privately developed launch vehicle to go into orbit.

The Falcon 1 was completely designed by SpaceX. It had two engines and was launched five times. On the last of these launches, it successfully delivered the Malaysian RazakSAT satellite into orbit. The rocket was then retired to make way for subsequent models (the Falcon 9, the Falcon Heavy and the Dragon) that had improved design features.

But the trajectory of SpaceX hasn't always been smooth. The first three test rockets each exploded before reaching orbit, leaving Musk with just enough money for one more try. It was fourth time lucky, or that was it: No one was going to invest in the company without at least one successful launch. Luckily for Musk, the Falcon made it up into orbit on that fourth occasion.

In June 2015 a SpaceX rocket resupplying the International Space Station exploded just two minutes after launch. The likely cause was a failed steel strut holding down a canister of helium. In theory, the strut in question was designed to withstand 10,000 pounds of force, but it failed with just 20 percent of that force. The rocket broke up into thousands of small parts, and the Dragon cargo capsule it was carrying fell into the sea, along with its 4,000 pounds of supplies. Had the Dragon been programmed with software to deploy its parachute, it might have survived, so the next-generation version (which is expected eventually to carry crew members into orbit) will have that software as well as its own thrusters. SpaceX is sending its own autonomous underwater vehicle to search for debris in a bid to better understand the cause of the accident and its impact on other parts of the craft.

 Don't overlook the small things.

The funding model for SpaceX is worth considering at this point. Although Musk did invest substantial amounts of his own fortune (an estimated $100 million by March 2006), he was by no means the only stakeholder. In 2008, $20 million in investment came from the Founders Fund (the venture-capital fund behind PayPal, Spotify, and Airbnb). The total budget of the company over the past 10 years has been in the region of $1 billion, the majority of which was income from development contracts. NASA alone has paid SpaceX somewhere in the region of $500 million. SpaceX has contracts for more than 40 space launches, and the company gains revenue from both down payments and ongoing progress payments as each stage of a project is completed. Musk has retained approximately two-thirds of the company's shares, an eye-watering sum given that in May 2012, after another successful flight, the company was valued at $2.8 billion.

> **"Failure is an option here. If things are not failing, you are not innovating enough."**
>
> —ELON MUSK

Although there has been much discussion in the marketplace about if and when SpaceX will have an IPO, Musk has stated that he plans to hold off until the Mars Colonial Transporter is flying regularly. In his own words, "I just don't want [SpaceX] to be controlled by some private-equity firm that would milk it for near-term revenue." Musk has no need to make a public offering of shares; SpaceX is a cash cow, and there are plenty of private customers eager to lap up shares without having them publicly traded. In January 2015, Google and Fidelity spent $1 billion buying 8.333 percent of the company, giving SpaceX a valuation of $12 billion.

For Musk, SpaceX is not just about the money. The challenge he has set for himself is what really excites him. Musk believes it is feasible to put the first human on Mars by 2021 and made this claim in an interview with *The Wall Street Journal* in 2011. What's more, he doesn't expect this to be a one-off achievement: In June 2015, he went one step further, telling Etv.com that by 2035 thousands of rockets will be flying to Mars each year, enabling us to establish a self-sustaining space colony with more than 1 million inhabitants.

SpaceX's low-cost launch model has put significant pressure on its competitors to lower their prices. An orbital launch from the Falcon Heavy costs just $1,000 per pound, spurring European competitor Arianespace to request subsidies from the European Union to remain competitive. In 2014, SpaceX won nine out of 20 worldwide bids for commercial launch services, more than any other company. SpaceX has signed contracts with the U.S. Air Force, NASA, and the Department of Defense in addition to its conventional commercial contracts.

TRANSPORTATION AND ENERGY

Tesla Motors

Tesla Motors takes its name and inspiration from the Serbian American physicist, electrical engineer, and inventor Nikola Tesla (1856–1943), who worked with Thomas Edison in New York and made major contributions to the modern alternating-current (AC) electricity supply system in his own right. The motor in the Tesla Roadster is based almost entirely on Tesla's original 1882 design.

 The best ideas aren't necessarily new ideas. Be prepared to take products or services that already exist and rework and improve them for the modern world.

As with PayPal, Musk was not the founder of Tesla Motors. That credit falls to engineer Martin Eberhard and his business partner, Marc Tarpenning. The pair founded Tesla Motors in summer 2003 with the principal aim of commercializing electric vehicles. They wanted to create first an aspirational sports car model to show off their technology, and then diversify into more mainstream, affordable models for ordinary families. Musk invested in Tesla in February 2004, joining the company as chairman of the board. He took an active interest in product development (though not in the day to day running of the business), and Eberhard credits Musk with the insistence on a carbon-fiber reinforced-polymer body, as well as the design of the power electronics module for the headlights.

 You don't always have to be the inventor!

Musk's investment in Tesla was in the region of $7.5 million (which came from his personal funds), making him the controlling investor in Tesla's first funding round. To any onlooker, this investment must have seemed crazy. The last successful automotive start-up in the U.S. was Chrysler in 1925, and no one had ever made money out of electric cars. The company looked like a money pit. Surely Musk wasn't just going to throw away everything he'd worked so hard to earn. Was he delusional?

Indeed, the early years of Tesla Motors were far from smooth. Although the company was picking up accolades, including for the Tesla Roadster the 2006 Global Green Product Award and the 2007 Index:Award, it was burning through funds at an alarming rate. Musk was forced to cut the size of his team by 10 percent in 2007 to stave off financial disaster, and the following year the Truth About Cars website launched a "Tesla Death Watch," anticipating the end was nigh. Valleywag, the Silicon Valley gossip blog, also marked Tesla as the number-one tech company fail of 2007. Thankfully for Musk, they had both underestimated his determination and the appeal of the Tesla product to investors.

People will always try to rain on your parade.
Keep your head down, keep working,
and ignore idle gossip.

Musk raised round after round of funding. He was confident and constantly enthused about Tesla and its potential, and investors believed what he had to say. He raised $45 million in May 2007, $40 million in December 2008, and a further $50 million from Germany's Daimler AG in May 2009. Musk had also contributed an estimated $70 million of his own money.

The company's fortunes began to take a turn for the better. Tesla delivered its first 147 cars by January 2009, demonstrating that they were a credible prospect. Abu Dhabi's Aabar Investments bought 40 percent of Daimler AG's interest in Tesla, and the company was advanced $465 million in loans from a Department of Energy program. Mainstream car manufacturers Ford and Nissan also received funds from this program, but Tesla was able to repay its loan well in advance of its competitors.

Tesla finally turned a profit for the first time in July 2009 on the back of sales of the Tesla Roadster. That month, 109 vehicles shipped, and as the company's fortunes now looked promising, Musk decided the time was right for an initial public offering. Tesla launched its IPO on the Nasdaq in June 2010. With a value of $17 each, 13,300,000 shares were issued, raising $226 million for the company. By the end of 2014, the share price had reached $240 per share, and the total value of the company was nearly $29 billion. Tesla was the top-performing company on the Nasdaq 100 index in 2013 and sold more than 33,000 cars worldwide in 2014.

Although Tesla's long-term goal is to produce cars for the mainstream consumer market, in the meantime it's having fun creating some top-end products that excite the automotive media. This shrewd business model creates aspiration, an appetite for Tesla's future products as they become affordable for ordinary, middle-class customers. Tesla's Model X SUV launched in September 2015 with a basic model costing around $80,000. If you wanted the top-of-the-line Signature Series, the price rose to at least $132,000. Unsurprisingly, the vehicle is exceptionally energy-efficient, but there are also a number of other interesting features: The car continually scans the road with camera, radar, and sonar systems so it can automatically brake before an accident and steer away from side collisions; the wing doors allow access in narrow spaces but also have sensors so they won't crunch up into the roof of a garage; and the car can do zero to 60 mph in 3.2 seconds. The Signature Series has a top speed of 275 mph.

> **"When Henry Ford made cheap, reliable cars, people said, 'Nah, what's wrong with a horse?' That was a huge bet he made, and it worked."**
>
> —ELON MUSK

Batteries

Tesla's innovations are not limited to the car market. Musk wants to bring affordable electrical energy into all facets of life. This is especially true regarding batteries. A Tesla battery is composed of thousands of lithium-ion cells typically used in laptops and small consumer electronic devices. Made by Panasonic (itself an investor in Tesla), the cells are small, lightweight, and cheap, costing around $200 per kWh, significantly less than any alternatives currently available.

Taking these batteries a step further, Tesla announced the Powerwall home battery packs in April 2015. The standard version is a 7 kWh wall-mounted unit, although industrial users can opt for far larger batteries in units of 100 kWh. Shifting suppliers enabled Tesla to cut costs by around 30 percent. The move into household energy storage is huge, because consumers with solar panels on their houses can, for the first time, actually store the energy they produce in a cost-effective manner. Bloomberg reported that Tesla consequently made $800 million on battery sales in the first week, smashing even Musk's expectations. Once it is operational, Musk's planned "gigafactory" in Nevada will enable Tesla to more than double the world's total annual production of lithium-ion batteries. He is taking on the energy market in a spectacular manner.

> **"There's a tremendous bias against taking risks. Everyone is trying to optimize their ass-covering."**
>
> —Elon Musk

Musk's interest in energy also lies in its production. SolarCity, one of the country's largest solar-power companies, designs, finances, and installs solar-power systems. It was founded in 2006 by two of Musk's cousins, Lyndon and Peter Rive, but Musk is SolarCity's chairman and provided its initial idea, as well as its start-up capital. SolarCity has a number of commercial solar installations in California, including on sites belonging to eBay, British Motors, Walmart, and Intel; it offers energy-efficiency evaluations and upgrades to homeowners; there is a five-year plan to build more than $1 billion in solar photovoltaic projects for military housing in the U.S.; it produced electric-car charging points; and it also installs snap-together solar panels. SolarCity plans to build a major new manufacturing facility in Buffalo, New York, for high-efficiency solar modules. When complete, this will be the largest such plant in the U.S. and will enable SolarCity to compete aggressively against manufacturers in China.

Supporting SolarCity—which now has a market capitalization in excess of $6 billion—is a good move for Musk, as it sits well with his investment in Tesla. Not only can SolarCity produce the quality car chargers Tesla needs, but the household batteries made by Tesla can also store electricity produced by homes with SolarCity's photovoltaic cells. It's a win-win situation.

 No market or business exists in isolation.

The Hyperloop

Musk's venture into public transportation, the Hyperloop, is as yet just an idea on the drawing board, but if his track record is anything to go by, even the most far-fetched idea might just come to fruition. The Hyperloop is basically a theoretical high-speed transportation system in which pressurized capsules ride on a cushion of air through reduced-pressure tubes. Musk proposed the system should run parallel to Interstate 5 between Los Angeles and San Francisco, a journey of 354 miles. He believes his system could cut the travel time to only 35 minutes, which would require an average speed of about 598 mph. Not only would this be significantly faster than even air travel, it would also substantially reduce traffic congestion and pollution on California's roads.

 Apply your expertise to real-world problems if you really want to have a positive impact.

Musk first proposed his idea for this "fifth mode of transport" in Santa Monica, California, in 2011. Addressing attendees at a tech

111

event, he spoke of his dream of a transportation option that was immune to bad weather, could not crash, had an average speed twice that of a typical jet, required little power, and could store energy for 24-hour operations. Musk envisaged his Hyperloop as a "cross between a Concorde and a rail gun and an air-hockey table."

The Hyperloop project faces significant, and expensive, technological challenges involving air resistance and friction. To see if he could make it work, Musk assembled a team of engineers from Tesla and SpaceX, who worked on the conceptual foundation and modeling and produced a white paper, inviting comment from the wider tech community. Unusually, their design was open source: Musk wanted anyone to be able to understand it and to contribute ideas for improvements. He then announced his plan to build a prototype to test the concept in practice and a design contest to gather suggestions.

To take his project to the next level, Musk is happy to have others contribute ideas. Hyperloop Transportation Technologies is a research company that uses crowdfunding and a collaborative approach to develop the system. More than 100 engineers, all of whom have taken stock options instead of upfront payment, are working together on designs and are expected to have their first feasibility study completed by the end of 2015; they admit, however, that they are at least 10 years away from opening a commercially viable Hyperloop. HTT hopes its IPO will raise $100 million to fund development. Permission has already been granted to build a five-mile test track alongside Interstate 5.

 You don't have to be possessive about your ideas. Commercial secrecy is an outdated model.

Musk has suggested a price tag of $6 billion for his own version of the Hyperloop, though critics do think this is optimistically low, and his alpha design outlines a scenario for the Hyperloop to cover its capital costs within 20 years. A one-way passenger ticket would be a very affordable $20 in this plan. The challenges are high—every critic is terrified of spiraling costs, while moving financial and political support away from California's other mega-project, a high-speed rail line that has many vested interests, is difficult.

AWARDS AND RECOGNITION

M usk's recognition is international in scope and touches on multiple disciplines. Even though he abandoned his own doctorate studies after only two days, other educational institutions have moved to recognize his contributions to technology. In the U.K., Surrey University (one of the world's foremost centers for the development of satellite technology) awarded Musk an honorary doctorate in aerospace engineering, and he also has a similar degree in engineering and technology from Yale. His third honorary doctorate, in design, comes from the ArtCenter College of Design in Pasadena, California.

Musk was asked to serve on the United States National Academy of Sciences Aeronautics and Space Engineering Board. He received the 2007–08 American Institute of Aeronautics and Astronautics George Low Award for his design of the Falcon 1, and the National Space Society's Von Braun Trophy and the Fédération Aéronautique Internationale's Gold Space Medal, both for this same achievement. The Kitty Hawk Foundation has designated Musk a Living Legend of Aviation, and in 2011 he received the Heinlein Prize for Advances in Space Commercialization.

Musk's lineup of business-world accolades is no less impressive. The magazines *R&D*, *Inc.*, and *Fortune* have all named him their entrepreneur of the year, while *Esquire* listed Musk as one of the 75 most influential people of the 21st century. In 2011, he appeared in *Forbes* magazine's list of America's 20 Most Powerful CEOs 40 and Under. If that weren't enough to confirm his superstar status, in January 2015 an episode of *The Simpsons* entitled "The Musk Who Fell to Earth" poked fun at some of his inventions. Musk made a guest appearance.

POLITICS AND BELIEFS

M usk has described himself as "half Democrat, half Republican...somewhere in the middle, socially liberal and fiscally conservative," and has contributed to election campaigns for both parties. The donations are linked to Musk's lobbying efforts on issues of importance to his companies. A report from the Sunlight Foundation found that SpaceX alone has spent $4 million lobbying both sides of Congress, and Musk himself has made $725,000 in campaign donations.

 When lobbying and making donations, focus on the causes that make most business sense.

Although Musk's own companies received government subsidies in the past, Musk subsequently spoke out against this. He believes a carbon tax levied on companies that are not environmentally friendly is a far better policy than costly subsidies. His view is controversial, however: Collectively, SpaceX, Tesla Motors, and SolarCity have benefited from an estimated $4.9 billion in government subsidies, and in their early days even these companies might not have succeeded without it.

In religion, Musk is a rationalist, basing his personal views on his understanding of the laws of physics. He thinks it is unlikely that religion and science can coexist. He does believe, however, that there is a significant chance that simple life exists on other planets, perhaps something akin to mold growing in a petri dish. Musk has "hope that there is other intelligent life in the known universe" and thinks that statistically it is "probably more likely than not."

What concerns Musk more is artificial intelligence, which he has called "the most serious threat to the survival of the human race." He is worried about its lack of regulatory oversight. When addressing the MIT AeroAstro Centennial Symposium, he said, "There have been movies about this, you know, like *Terminator*— there are some scary outcomes. And we should try to make sure the outcomes are good, not bad."

 If there is something out there that worries you or that you fear, be honest about it.

PERSONAL LIFE

Musk met his first wife, Justine, while they were both students at Queen's University in Ontario. She was an aspiring writer, and he wooed her with ice cream and bunches of roses. She traveled to Japan to teach but returned to the U.S. to join Musk in Silicon Valley, and the couple married in January 2000. The board of X.com urged the bride and groom to sign a postnuptial agreement to protect Musk's newly acquired wealth, and the sense of economic inequality within the relationship, combined with Musk's alpha-male tendencies, caused notable strain.

 The characteristics that make you successful in business will not necessarily serve you well in other aspects of your life.

Nothing could have prepared the Musks for the trauma to come, however. Their first son, Nevada Alexander, was born in 2002. The same week Musk sold PayPal, catapulting his wealth to in excess of $100 million, the 10-week-old baby was put down for a nap and stopped breathing. Although he was resuscitated by paramedics, Nevada had been deprived of oxygen for too long and was brain-dead. Three days later, his life support machines were turned off. The cause of death was sudden infant death syndrome.

Musk bottled up his emotions, refusing to talk with his wife about their loss. At first, Justine grieved openly, but Musk decried this behavior as "emotionally manipulative," so she was forced to hide her pain. Despite being caught in a spiral of depression, she returned to the IVF clinic and gave birth first to twins and then to triplets, five boys in all. Griffin and Xavier were born in 2004, and Damian, Saxon, and Kai followed in 2006.

On the face of it, the Musks had a perfect family setup and social life. They lived in a 6,000-square-foot house in the Bel Air Hills; partied with Bono, Paris Hilton, and Leonardo DiCaprio; and traveled everywhere by private jet. What was missing was intimacy and mutual respect. Musk was obsessed with his work and paid little attention to his wife. Justine had sacrificed her successful literary career to raise their children and support him, but he was dismissive. An intelligent, capable woman, she had been reduced to little more than a trophy wife, and she understandably resented that fact.

Faced with a collapsing marriage and a wife who craved equality in their partnership, Musk agreed to begin marriage counseling. He lasted just three sessions, then impatiently issued Justine an ultimatum: fix their marriage that day or divorce the next. No relationship can be rebuilt in a day, and Musk filed for divorce the next morning. The divorce, in spring 2008, was messy. Although Justine had earlier signed away her rights, including those to communal property, there was some debate as to whether Musk had fully disclosed his finances at the time of signing, which was a marital fiduciary duty. Resolution became a matter for the courts.

Just six weeks after Musk filed for divorce, he announced his engagement to British actress Talulah Riley. The couple married in 2010, and their marriage lasted two years. The *Telegraph* reported that Riley received a $4.2 million divorce settlement, but the couple reconciled, albeit temporarily, in 2014. Another split occurred on December 31, 2014, and their divorce was finalized in 2016.

PHILANTHROPY

Despite payouts to his ex-wives, Musk still has ample fortune to spend, and he distributes some of it philanthropically through his Musk Foundation, which provides solar-energy systems to communities hit by natural disasters. His donations have included a 25 kW solar-power system for the South Bay Community Alliance's hurricane response center in Alabama and a $250,000 contribution toward a solar-power project in a tsunami-affected area of Japan.

Musk has also made donations to individual projects, including $1 million toward the construction of the Tesla Science Center at the scientist's former Wardenclyffe Laboratory on Long Island, New York, as well as a pledge to build a Tesla Supercharger in the museum's car park. He gave $10 million to the Future of Life Institute to fund its global research program to try to ensure that artificial intelligence remains beneficial, while Musk's Xprize Foundation holds competitions to encourage technological developments that benefit humanity.

> **"I wouldn't say I have a lack of fear. In fact, I'd like my fear emotion to be less because it's very distracting and fries my nervous system."**
>
> —Elon Musk

CONCLUSION

Unlike a politician, Musk is not answerable to an electorate. He doesn't have to make populist choices, and he can take on projects whose results won't be seen until quite some time down the line. He is also not like other businessmen. His companies do have shareholders, of course, but he is prepared to put his own money into a project to test it out and get things up and running to the point where the idea is proven and other investors want to jump onto his bandwagon. He sees his role in life as not just about making money—though he does have a competitive, acquisitive side—but also about addressing the major issues humanity faces, challenges that seem so huge and insurmountable that others are afraid to even try.

Perhaps Musk's greatest, most admirable asset is that he can look at the big picture and take the long view. He's not in a rush, and he doesn't have to prove himself to others. His achievements to date already put him on a level far beyond what most other entrepreneurs or inventors can ever hope to achieve, so what Musk does now is entirely up to him. This gives him a great deal of freedom to try things out, and the freedom to think and dream is something all of his disciples can emulate. We may be restrained by physical or financial barriers, but that doesn't mean we can't open our minds and look at our challenges in new and imaginative ways. When our thoughts are unencumbered, we will come up with our best solutions.

Musk's life and work so far also teach us that you don't have to be a specialist in one narrow field: a true Renaissance man like Leonardo da Vinci, Musk can think creatively, and excel, in multiple disciplines. Yes, he has undoubtedly mastered the basics of mathematics, physics, engineering, and computer programming, not to mention public speaking, leadership, and self-promotion, but he is not (yet) a Nobel Prize–winning scientist, and his oratory skills fall far short of, let's say, Winston Churchill's.

What Musk does have is a breadth of interest and knowledge, enough to understand the complexities of arguments and the nuances of details presented to him. He is perpetually curious, even to the point of obsession, wanting to know more and more. He has learned to surround himself with the greatest thinkers and doers in each industry he wants to work in. He inspires and leads them but depends very much on their collective input and expertise to make his projects happen. Musk's mastery of the dual arts of leadership and delegation is what enables him to rise above his competitors, to see further, and to achieve far more.

It would be possible to replicate Musk's educational and professional career moves step-by-step without achieving the same outcome. He is, like any successful entrepreneur, the beneficiary of a particular fortunate set of circumstances. Had he made the same decisions, the same bids, at a different time in his career, the outcomes could have been very different: We have already seen how close SpaceX and Tesla Motors came to falling flat on their faces. The final lesson we should learn from Musk, then, is that what determines success is not your qualifications, where you were born, or how much money you have. Instead, it is how you choose to see the world, your openness to ideas, and how you respond to opportunities and challenges when you are faced with them. No one in this world, not even Elon Musk, gets through life with a completely easy ride. For all of us, there are forks in the road and vital decisions to be made. We must approach these times with confidence and conviction if we are to achieve our goals.

Mark
Zuckerberg

INTRODUCTION

Unless you've buried your head in the sand for the past decade, you cannot have missed the social-media phenomenon that is Facebook. It has an estimated 1.5 billion users, from nearly every corner of the globe, and is the driving force behind Free Basics, an app that provides free internet services in the developing world.

Its young founder, Mark Zuckerberg, has not only made exorbitant wealth but also positioned himself at the forefront of enterprise and innovation. He has been named *Time* magazine's man of the year and is the poster child for the tech world. In this chapter, you will find five unforgettable lessons drawn from Zuckerberg's life and work, which you can apply in your own life. Though not all of these will be personally applicable, you can take inspiration from them, and put into practice those that are most relevant to you.

CHILDHOOD AND EDUCATION

Mark Zuckerberg was a child prodigy, a fascinating, precocious boy with a seemingly infinite capacity to learn and innovate. Born on May 14, 1984, in White Plains, New York, the son of dentist Edward Zuckerberg and psychiatrist Karen Kempner, Mark and his three sisters were raised in New York State and New Hampshire.

All the Zuckerbergs were academically gifted and professional high-achievers, and Mark was no exception. At Phillips Exeter Academy, an independent boarding and day school, Zuckerberg followed in the footsteps of numerous notable alumni, including Dan Brown, author of *The Da Vinci Code*; Lloyd Shapley, winner of the 2012 Nobel Prize in Economics; and Adam D'Angelo, computer scientist and cofounder of the billion-dollar Q&A website Quora. Zuckerberg won academic prizes in math, astronomy, physics, and classical studies; was captain of the fencing team; and by the time he applied to Harvard University, he could read and write French, Hebrew, Latin, and ancient Greek, in addition to his native English.

Zuckerberg's interest in computer programming started while he was in middle school. He learned Atari BASIC programming from his father, then took private classes with software developer David Newman. While still in high school, Zuckerberg enrolled in a graduate class at Mercy College in New York and built a number of programs, including computer games with artwork designed by his friends; ZuckNet, a precursor to AOL's Instant Messenger (released a year later), which enabled all the computers in his house to communicate with those in his father's dental office; and the Synapse Media Player, which employed machine learning to analyze and predict users' listening preferences. Synapse Media Player was featured in both *Slashdot* and *PC Magazine,* where it received a rating of 3/5 from reviewers.

Zuckerberg enrolled at Harvard, signing up for classes in computer science and psychology. He belonged to the Alpha Epsilon Pi fraternity, which is based upon Jewish principles (Zuckerberg was raised Jewish), and notable members have included Nobel Prize winners, Olympic athletes, attorneys general, filmmakers, entrepreneurs, and even the inventor of Tinder. This network would stand Zuckerberg in good stead as he pursued his own commercial ambitions. He also belonged to Kirkland House, an undergraduate residence popular with Harvard's athletes.

Although Zuckerberg was doubtless academically able and passionate about his subjects, he did not complete his degree. He decided to take a semester off from studying to concentrate on developing Facebook, then dropped out of the university entirely to devote his full attention to the company's growth.

FACEBOOK

Zuckerberg became accomplished at computer programming at an early age and saw it as a means of entertainment as much as something with commercial value. The programming skills he learned in his teenage years and honed at Harvard, where they were encouraged and inspired by his fellow students, set him on the path to developing what is financially the most successful social-media platform in the world.

Early Experiments

As a sophomore, Zuckerberg created CourseMatch, a simple program that enabled users to select courses (informed by the choices of other users) and to form study groups. It was his first attempt at social networking and, though not terribly exciting, it laid the groundwork for his next project, Facemash.

 Spend time experimenting with your ideas so that you hone your skills, and be prepared to rework them.

A computerized variant of the "Hot or Not?" game, Facemash was the work of Zuckerberg and three of his friends: Andrew McCollum, Chris Hughes, and Dustin Moskovitz. Zuckerberg took images from the online "face books" (or student profiles) of nine Harvard residence halls and laid them side by side in pairs. Users could then vote as to who was hot and who was not. Zuckerberg launched the site on October 28, 2003, but had no ownership of the content: The photos in the original face books were intended for reference only, to help students identify one another. Zuckerberg had to hack the Harvard server in order to collect the pictures for his site.

Facemash was an immediate hit. Zuckerberg forwarded it to several Harvard servers one weekend, and by Monday it had to be shut down because its popularity had overwhelmed one of the network switches. When what he had done was discovered, Zuckerberg faced charges of breach of security and violating copyright and individual privacy; he faced expulsion from the university, but the charges against him were later dropped.

Not one to let the site go entirely, however, he reformatted it for his art-history final, uploading 500 Augustan images and allowing classmates to share their notes in the comments section alongside each image. According to Zuckerberg's art-history professor, the project had the best grades of any final he had ever given. This was Zuckerberg's first social hack.

> **"All of my friends who have younger siblings who are going to college or high school—my number-one piece of advice is: You should learn how to program."**
>
> —Mark Zuckerberg

The Birth of Facebook

His experience with Facemash taught Zuckerberg several important things. Interviewed in *The Harvard Crimson,* he said, "Everyone's been talking a lot about a universal face book within Harvard. I think it's kind of silly that it would take the university a couple of years to get around to it, as I can do it better than they can, and I can do it in a week."

He was aware of a need in the marketplace and knew he had the skills to fulfill it; if he could do it faster than anyone else, he would have the advantage. Zuckerberg wanted to create a website that would allow members of the university not only to see students' images and profiles but also to connect with one another. The idea for Facebook was born.

 The very best ideas are simple.

Zuckerberg started coding Facebook in January 2004. Unsure of how to promote his new site, he asked his friends for advice. Moskovitz, his roommate, has recounted Facebook's entrance into the world. "When Mark finished the site, he told a couple of friends ... then one of them suggested putting it on the Kirkland House online mailing list, which was ... 300 people," he said. "By the end of the night, we were ... actively watching the registration process. Within 24 hours, we had somewhere between 1,200 and 1,500 registrants."

"The Facebook," as it was then known, was an instant hit, but it was not without problems. Three of Zuckerberg's fellow students at Harvard—Cameron Winklevoss; Cameron's twin brother, Tyler Winklevoss; and Divya Narendra,—all accused Zuckerberg of agreeing to help them build a social network called Harvard Connection and then running off with their idea. They took their complaint to *The Harvard Crimson,* and an investigation began.

Zuckerberg was not about to sit by blindly; he wanted to know what was going on so he would be in a stronger position to respond. Using the Facebook, he was able to identify users who also worked at *The Harvard Crimson.* He cross-referenced their names with the list of failed logins to the Facebook, then used those same passwords to try to access the users' Harvard email accounts. He successfully accessed two and read their communications as the investigation progressed. Three of the users subsequently brought a lawsuit against Zuckerberg for this abuse of trust and breach of privacy, but the case was settled.

When the Facebook was launched, you had to have a Harvard email address to sign up. This was a shrewd move, as a social network can work only if it has sufficient penetration within a group. People will join only if their friends have already joined or if they expect to find people they know, and this is far easier to achieve if the pool of people is small. In the first month after the Facebook was launched, half of Harvard's undergraduate population had signed up. The appetite for the site was proven, and its model was working.

Founders

Up to this point, the Facebook was more or less a one-man band. It was Zuckerberg's baby, but he wasn't arrogant: He knew that in order for the project to grow and realize its full potential, he had to bring other people on board. He recruited four colleagues from his Harvard social circle to help him develop and promote the Facebook further.

 Launch your products in a market you understand.

Each of Zuckerberg's recruits had his own area of expertise and responsibility. Eduardo Saverin, a Brazilian student who was president of the Harvard Investment Association, had already proven his business skills by making a $300,000 profit from strategic investments in the Brazilian oil industry. He became the Facebook's chief financial officer and business manager. It was Saverin's money, along with Zuckerberg's, that sustained the company during its first few months, and both men took equity stakes.

Zuckerberg's roommate, Dustin Moskovitz, who had been watching the night Zuckerberg launched the Facebook, came on board as a programmer. He was the company's first chief technology officer and then vice president of engineering. In March 2011 *Forbes* magazine would declare him the youngest self-made billionaire in history. He was just 28 years old.

Andrew McCollum did the graphic-design work. He was at the company for its first three years, then returned to Harvard to complete his undergraduate degree and then a master's.

The final member of this founding team was Chris Hughes, who had met Zuckerberg during his freshman year in 2002 and had beta-tested many of Zuckerberg's early designs, as well as making product suggestions. Hughes became the Facebook's spokesman, and it was his idea to open the site to more schools, paving the way for its global expansion.

THE GROWTH OF FACEBOOK

In March 2004, Zuckerberg's site was opened up to students at Columbia, Stanford, and Yale Universities. The utility of the network, combined with its sense of exclusivity—you had to be at one of these elite schools to join—made it instantly popular.

 Exclusivity is a powerful marketing tool, as you can create demand for a product before it is even available.

Zuckerberg and his colleagues traveled to Palo Alto, in the center of Silicon Valley, in summer 2004. They incorporated the Facebook as a company, and Sean Parker, cofounder of the file-sharing site Napster, became its first president. He had already been advising Zuckerberg informally for some time, and he convinced him and his colleagues to remain in California (aside from Hughes, who returned to Harvard; he later rejoined the company after graduation, in 2006). Venture capitalist Peter Thiel, who had made his money as the cofounder of

PayPal alongside Elon Musk, made a $500,000 angel investment in the Facebook in exchange for a 10.2 percent equity stake. Other seed-round investments were made by Reid Hoffman, CEO of LinkedIn; entrepreneur Mark Pincus, who had sold his first start-up, Freeloader, Inc., for $38 million and would later found online games company Zynga; and Maurice Werdegar of Western Technology Investment.

> **"The Hacker Way is an approach to building that involves continuous improvement and iteration. Hackers believe that something can always be better and that nothing is ever complete."**
>
> —Mark Zuckerberg

The Facebook really took off in 2005. The company now had its base in Palo Alto, where tech entrepreneurs and investors were a dime a dozen, yet all were excited about Zuckerberg's idea. He dropped *the* from the company's name and branched out to serve 21 universities in the United Kingdom (Oxford and Cambridge first among them, in keeping with the idea that this was a network for elite university students and alumni). An invitation-only version for high schools was launched, and additional networks were created for the employees of Apple, Microsoft, and other major tech companies. By the end of the year, Facebook was available to more than 2,000 colleges and universities and 25,000 high schools in the United States and Canada, the United Kingdom and Ireland, Australia and New Zealand, and Mexico. The company raised $12.7 million in venture capital from Accel Partners, valuing Facebook at $98 million.

In summer 2006, Facebook was open to anyone around the world, as long as they were age 13 and older and had a valid email address. Zuckerberg closed Facebook's series-B funding round with investments from Greylock Partners and Meritech Capital, as well as additional funds from Thiel and Accel. The valuation of Facebook stood at $500 million—not bad for 18 months' work.

Sales Negotiations and Profitability

Facebook had grown very quickly, and it seemed inevitable that Zuckerberg and his cofounders would want to realize their investment and sell out at least part of their stakes as soon as possible. Facebook's main competitor, MySpace, was sold to Rupert Murdoch's News Corporation in 2005, and market analysts thought Zuckerberg would avail himself of a similar exit strategy. In quick succession, however, Zuckerberg turned down a $750 million offer from an unknown bidder and a $1 billion offer from Yahoo! Microsoft suggested it would make a $300 million-to-$500 million investment in exchange for a 5 percent stake, and Google followed suit. But Zuckerberg wasn't interested. He wanted to keep Facebook independent, stating, "We're not really looking to sell the company.... We're not looking to IPO anytime soon. It's just not the core focus of the company."

> **"I literally coded Facebook in my dorm room and launched it from my dorm room. I rented a server for $85 a month, and I funded it by putting an ad on the side, and we've funded ever since by putting ads on the side."**
>
> —MARK ZUCKERBERG

His view may well have been shaped by the fact that Thiel had already created an internal valuation of $8 billion for Facebook, based on its predicted revenues. Microsoft was allowed to invest $240 million for a 1.6 percent stake, implying a valuation of $15 billion, and Hong Kong billionaire Li Ka-shing invested a further $60 million.

The interesting thing is that all of these investments were speculative: Facebook had a huge network of users, but they paid no subscription fees, and the site generated almost no revenue. Zuckerberg was open about his failure to monetize the site, saying, "I don't think social networks can be monetized in the same way that search did.... In three years from now, we have to figure out what the optimum model is. But that is not our primary focus today."

For Facebook's board members, however, monetization was a priority. The board recruited Sheryl Sandberg, vice president of global online sales and operations at Google, as Facebook's chief operating officer in 2008. Zuckerberg had known Sandberg for just a few months, having met her first at a Christmas party and again at the World Economic Forum in Davos, Switzerland, but he was convinced she was the perfect fit for the role. He wasn't wrong.

 A company has to make a profit. That is its purpose.

Sandberg was the first woman in a senior role at Facebook. She recognized that the company was "primarily interested in building a really cool site; profits, they assumed, would follow." But Sandberg decided a more proactive approach was required. She brainstormed ideas with Facebook employees and concluded that advertising revenues would be the main source of monetization. The board agreed with her, and Sandberg changed the company's advertising model. As a result, Facebook had positive cash flow for the first time, in September 2009.

Acquisitions

Once Facebook became profitable, it was in a position to start investing in other companies and make wholesale acquisitions.

These were usually for competing products or services that could enrich Facebook's portfolio and technical capacity.

Examples of early acquisitions included FriendFeed, a real-time news-feed aggregator that brought together user feeds from multiple social-media platforms, blogs, etc. It was the brainchild of Bret Taylor (co-creator of Google Maps) and Paul Buchheit (lead developer of Gmail, who also prototyped Google AdSense). Others were Octazen Solutions, a Malaysian start up whose software could be used to import contacts from various sources; the photo-sharing system Divvyshot; and the team behind Storylane, a start-up that allowed users to share interests with a given community.

Such acquisitions made Facebook increasingly attractive to investors. After its IPO, in February 2012, Facebook had a much larger pool of cash to draw from, and the board decided to make two further, phenomenal, acquisitions: Instagram and WhatsApp, Inc.

 Buy into other companies that enhance your core offering.

The photo-and-video-sharing social network Instagram was released in October 2010. Its square, Polaroid-style images were distinctive (though in later versions of the app, alternative aspect ratios were also popular), and users liked being able to add filters to their pictures. The free app had 100 million users in its first 18 months, and in April 2012, Facebook acquired Instagram for $1 billion in cash and stock. It was a shrewd investment: Instagram trebled its number of users over the next two-year period, a rate of growth even Facebook itself could not match.

Although Facebook paid a gargantuan sum for Instagram, it shelled out even more money for the messaging service WhatsApp. Created by two former employees of Yahoo!, who, ironically enough, had been turned down for jobs at Facebook,

WhatsApp launched in November 2009. By spring 2014, it had 500 million users a month and ultimately reached around 1 billion. Facebook acquired WhatsApp in February 2014 for $19 billion, of which $4 billion was paid in cash, $12 billion in Facebook shares, and $3 billion in restricted stock options for WhatsApp's founders.

Immediately after the WhatsApp acquisition, Zuckerberg gave the keynote address at the Mobile World Congress in Barcelona. He explained that the move was a key component of his vision for Internet.org, which he later discussed in an interview with TechCrunch. The idea, he said, was "to develop a group of basic internet services that would be free of charge to use—'a 911 for the internet.' These could be a social-networking service like Facebook, a messaging service, maybe search, and other things like weather. Providing a bundle of these free of charge to users will work like a gateway drug of sorts—users who may be able to afford data services and phones these days just don't see the point of why they would pay for those data services. This would give them some context for why they are important, and that will lead them to paying for more services like this—or so the hope goes."

 Even if you think your ideas are good, you need to be able to explain them in a cohesive, convincing way to other people.

After making its deal with Facebook, WhatsApp developed the ability to handle voice calls and dropped its annual $1 subscription charge. Both of these changes increased its appeal to customers, with *Forbes* magazine predicting that WhatsApp and Skype would cause conventional communications companies to lose a total of $386 billion between 2012 and 2018. Facebook and its subsidiaries once again were changing the ways we communicate and make money.

Initial Public Offering

Despite Zuckerberg's early resistance to the idea of an IPO, it was inevitable that Facebook would one day have a public share offering: No single company could afford to buy Facebook entirely, yet the investors had somehow to realize their investment.

Zuckerberg's leadership and his conviction about the potential of Facebook was essential, because they enabled him to grow the company to well beyond its estimated size and the valuation offered by Yahoo!, Microsoft, and Google. His confidence and his direct involvement in the product paid off. By assembling a world-class team, he gained the largest valuation for a newly public company at the time. Facebook's IPO raised $16 billion, making it the third largest in U.S. history.

So how did it happen? What steps did Zuckerberg take? By resisting both buyouts and taking the company public for a protracted period, Zuckerberg was able to grow Facebook (increasing its ultimate valuation) and create an appetite in the marketplace for its shares. Numerous investors wanted a piece of the action but couldn't buy in, and this made the company even more tantalizing. He told *PC Magazine* in 2010, "We are definitely in no rush."

 Bide your time.

On February 1, 2012, Zuckerberg filed Facebook's S1 document with the U.S. Securities and Exchange Commission. Key points of the document were an outline of the company's position at the time (845 million active monthly users, 2.7 billion daily likes and comments, and an increasing but decelerating increase in the number of users and income); a statement that Zuckerberg would retain 22 percent of Facebook's shares but 57 percent of the voting shares; and an indication that Facebook expected to raise $5 billion from the IPO.

Zuckerberg personally led the road show for the IPO, and he did it in his own inimitable way. He turned up at the first investors' meeting wearing a hoodie, not a suit, which caused consternation in more conservative business circles and generated plenty of column inches. Perhaps that was the idea. One investor described the move (which may or may not have been deliberate) as a "mark of immaturity," but it could also be seen as Zuckerberg reminding would-be investors that the ball was in his court, and he would run the road show and the IPO as he saw fit. He didn't need the money and therefore had the power.

 You need to strike a careful balance between being yourself and doing what investors and customers expect.

Valuations of Facebook fluctuated significantly during this period, though overall they increased. The low initial estimate was $28 to $35 per share, but this was quickly revised up to $34 to $38 per share. This top estimate gave a total valuation for the company of $104 billion, yet there was still strong demand from would-be investors, especially from retail investors. The previous strong performance of Google and LinkedIn gave investors confidence, and no one wanted to risk missing out.

Two days before the IPO, Zuckerberg announced that, due to high demand, 25 percent more shares would be released. The stock debuted with 421 million shares. Some analysts did express concern, thinking the estimates overvalued Facebook, especially given worries about the company's advertising model: Just days before the IPO, General Motors announced publicly it was going to cancel its $10 million advertising campaign on Facebook due to underperformance.

The Facebook IPO was fascinating to watch, as it was a cultural event as much as a business one. Reuters declared it a "cultural phenomenon," and Zuckerberg, ever the showman, ran a series of events in the run-up to it. The night before, he led an all-night hackathon; CBS coined the word *Zuckonomics* to describe the way in which the IPO was playing out; and Zuckerberg rang a bell in the Facebook campus's Hackers Square to announce, in time-honored fashion, that the company was going public.

Trading in Facebook shares was due to begin at 11 A.M. on May 18, 2012, but it was delayed by half an hour due to technical issues at Nasdaq. This didn't bode well, as there were to be technical glitches throughout the day, and buyers couldn't always see whether their trades had been successful. The opening share price had been set at $38 and shot up as high as $45, but Facebook couldn't maintain this price. When it fell below $38, the underwriters had to wade in to keep the price steady, and the day's trading closed with a disappointing share price of just $38.23. The stock did set a new record for the trading volume of an IPO (460 million shares), and it raised $16 billion. The IPO confirmed Zuckerberg's own stake as being worth $19 billion, so all in all, it wasn't a bad day for him.

 Be prepared to be pleasantly surprised on some occasions and sorely disappointed on others.

In the two weeks following the IPO, Facebook's share price decreased. Trading curbs were used to slow the decline, but Facebook closed its first full week of trading down at $31.91, and after two weeks the share price was just $27.72. It would be four weeks before the company made a modest gain, and when The *Wall Street Journal* described the IPO as a fiasco, it wasn't the only one holding that opinion. More than 40 legal suits against

Facebook's lead underwriters, Morgan Stanley, JP Morgan, and Goldman Sachs, followed, with Morgan Stanley being forced to settle allegations of improperly influencing research analysts for $5 million. The botched IPO damaged the reputation of both Morgan Stanley (the primary underwriter) and Nasdaq.

Those investors who did keep their Facebook shares (and their nerve) rather than dumping them in panic and fury, made a shrewd decision. The share price grew consistently since hitting an all-time low of $18.06 in August 2012. Facebook was expected to outperform the market in subsequent years, and six years later, its price approached $200. It seems the IPO wasn't such a fiasco after all.

 You need to be in business for the long haul.

Legal Disputes

The extraordinary success of Facebook and the wealth the company generated for Zuckerberg have meant, perhaps inevitably, that plenty of people are extremely jealous of what he has received. Some of them believe they are entitled to a slice of the Facebook pie because of their early involvement or ideas; others are just trying their luck. In either case, such individuals were canny enough to realize that whether their claims were valid or not, simply making allegations would likely catapult them into the limelight, giving them their 30 seconds of fame. For the Winklevoss brothers, that period lasted longer, though it didn't exactly show them in a good light.

From the week of Facebook's launch until June 2008, Zuckerberg was at loggerheads with twins Cameron and Tyler Winklevoss and their classmate Divya Narendra, all three of whom had studied together at Harvard. The plaintiffs alleged that they had hired Zuckerberg in 2003 to help them build a campus dating site called Harvard Connection but that he had stalled their project and ultimately stolen their idea and turned it into Facebook. Zuckerberg filed a countersuit, accusing the plaintiffs of unfair business practices, and the case was settled out of court.

 Be prepared for people you have worked with in the past to turn against you when you start to taste success.

But the story doesn't end there. The settlement was based on stock and, by extension, Facebook's valuation. The plaintiffs argued that Zuckerberg had fraudulently misrepresented the value of Facebook stock and took him back to court. It was a public-relations nightmare, one that Zuckerberg surely thought he had seen the end of. Thankfully for him, Judge James Ware of Federal District Court in San Jose sided with Zuckerberg, enforcing the earlier decision. The judge noted that the plaintiffs were upset that Facebook's valuation was not the $15 billion that recent media reports had suggested but that Facebook's own valuation was fair. He also suggested that the Winklevoss twins' father, Howard, was the main force behind the dispute.

The Winklevosses and Narendra took their handout and slunk away, and Facebook issued the following statement: "The ConnectU founders [i.e., the Winklevosses] understood the deal they made, and we are gratified that the court rejected their false allegations of fraud. Their challenge was simply a case of 'buyer's remorse,' as described by the Boston court earlier this month. We were disappointed that we had to litigate the settlement, as we believed we were caught in the middle of a fee dispute between ConnectU's founders and its former counsel. Nevertheless, we can now consider this chapter closed and wish the Winklevoss brothers the best of luck in their future endeavors."

When you win, be gracious and humble.

The Winklevoss twins were not the only people to claim Zuckerberg had acted in a less than honorable fashion. Facebook cofounder Eduardo Saverin had a claim to make too, and in his case it was more valid. In addition to putting his own money into the project, Saverin was Facebook's first chief financial officer and business manager. In 2012, *Business Insider* magazine obtained a private email sent by Zuckerberg suggesting that he had knowingly cut Saverin out of Facebook in 2005 and diluted his stake in the company. Saverin's exit was central to the plot of the 2010 film *The Social Network,* but not even the film's writers could have anticipated this particular turn of events.

Saverin made it clear to Zuckerberg that, as Saverin would be the only shareholder diluted by the grants issuances, he would have a legitimate claim to accuse Facebook of breaching its fiduciary duty, and he recommended that, to avoid this, Zuckerberg should get Saverin's consent for the issuances in writing. Zuckerberg did not heed this advice, and Saverin successfully sued Facebook for approximately 5 percent of the company. At the IPO, that stake was work around $5 billion.

 ## Treat those you work with fairly.

A number of smaller lawsuits were also brought against Facebook by users and their representatives. Decided in 2010, *Lane v. Facebook* was a class-action challenge to Facebook's privacy settings. When the company launched Beacon (which broadcast users' purchases from Facebook's affiliate sites), the default privacy settings required users to opt out, rather than in. Many users were unaware of this, and as their purchases were then broadcast to their social and professional networks via their

Facebook news feed, they felt their privacy had been breached. The lawyers representing the plaintiffs claimed Facebook had broken the Electronic Communications Privacy Act, the Video Privacy Protection Act, and the California Consumer Legal Remedies Act, as well as violating the California Computer Crime Law and the Computer Fraud and Abuse Act. Facebook denied wrongdoing but established a cash settlement fund of $9.5 million. This was used to open and run a privacy foundation designed to educate users. Facebook terminated the Beacon program, paid the lawyers' fees, and made small compensation payments ($1,000 to $15,000) to the class representatives.

> **"When I was in college, I did a lot of stupid things, and I don't want to make an excuse for that. Some of the things that people accuse me of are true; some of them aren't."**
>
> —MARK ZUCKERBERG

Facebook has collaborated with academics to conduct a number of experiments on its users. These include "A 61-Million-Person Experiment in Social Influence and Political Mobilization," which Facebook ran during the 2010 U.S. presidential election, and "Emotional Contagion Through Social Networks," a controversial 2014 study that manipulated the balance of positive and negative messages seen by 700,000 users. The study was criticized for its ethics, causing the watchdog group Electronic Privacy Information Center to file a formal complaint with the Federal Trade Commission. It alleged Facebook had conducted the study without the knowledge or consent of its users and secretly conducted a psychological experiment on their emotions, thus breaching their privacy. Law professor James Grimmelmann stated that he believed the action was "illegal, immoral, and mood-altering."

INTERNET.ORG

With billions of dollars in personal wealth, not to mention command of the Facebook platform, Zuckerberg has to decide what his legacy will be. He's only in his 30s and will unlikely be inclined, or able, to replicate the commercial success of Facebook, but that doesn't mean he can't make world-altering changes in other fields, including philanthropy. Potentially more far-reaching, however, is his Internet.org initiative.

A partnership between Facebook and Ericsson, MediaTek, Nokia, Opera Software, Qualcomm, and Samsung, Internet.org was launched in August 2013, and Zuckerberg issued a 10-page white paper and gave a detailed video interview with Tech-Crunch elaborating on the idea.

Zuckerberg believes that "connectivity is a human right" and that basic web servers should be available worldwide for free. The first Internet.org summit was held in October 2014 in India, where Zuckerberg met with Indian prime minister Narendra Modi to discuss the project. Internet.org provides free internet services through an app called Free Basics. Although it is an admirable initiative at face value, with much to recommend it, it has its detractors, and their concerns do have some basis.

First, critics have argued that Internet.org violates net neutrality. Facebook is, in essence, an unregulated gatekeeper to the Free Basics platform, deciding which services will be provided on it. Facebook's rivals might well be discriminated against. More than a dozen countries have offered Free Basics, delivering it through approved mobile-network providers. The service was launched in India in October 2015, but Zuckerberg was accused, perhaps unfairly, of targeting India's poor with Facebook proxies. The Telecom Regulatory Authority of India banned the service in the country just a year after its launch, on the grounds that Free Basics' commercials were misleading and had masked the identity of its supporters in a manner called "astroturfing."

 You need to tread carefully with regulatory bodies, thoroughly researching their authority and building relationships with their decision makers.

The Internet.org project has brought more than an estimated 19 million new internet users online. Kids can do their homework and enhance their education; entrepreneurs can establish, expand, and market their businesses; and millions more people can learn about health, their rights, and the world around them. Any app can be offered on the platform as long as it meets Free Basics' guidelines, granting developers access to vast new markets in the developing world.

WEALTH

In December 2015, *Business Inside* magazine estimated Zuckerberg's personal wealth (including his shareholding in Facebook) at $46 billion. He made nearly $12 billion of that wealth in 2015 alone. As his salary from Facebook was just $1 a year, this increase was driven almost entirely by Facebook's rising share price, though he has also made personal investments in companies such as Mastery Connect ($5 million), AltSchool ($100 million), Vicarious ($52 million), and Panorama Education ($4 million). Since 2010, *Time* magazine has declared him one of the 100 wealthiest and most influential people in the world, and his income stream looks as though it will only increase in the coming years.

AWARDS AND ACCOLADES

Unusually for a virtuosic billionaire, Zuckerberg hasn't actively courted awards and accolades. He has been satisfied to be allowed to run his company the way he wants and to generate vast sums of money doing so. But awards have come his way, since his achievements are so remarkable they cannot be ignored. In 2010, he was named the Person of the Year by *Time* magazine, and *The Jerusalem Post* followed up with a similar accolade the following year, adding him to its Most Influential Jews list. In 2016, Zuckerberg was nominated as CEO of the Year at the 9th Annual Crunchies Awards, TechCrunch's recognition of leaders in the tech field; he won despite stiff competition from Tim Cook (Apple), Jack Dorsey (Twitter/Square), Susan Wojcicki (YouTube), and Elon Musk (Tesla).

For a self-proclaimed geek like Zuckerberg, however, one of his proudest moments is likely to be his cameo appearance on *The Simpsons*. In the "Loan-a-Lisa" episode, Lisa takes Nelson to a startup event to meet successful founders, in the hope that they will inspire him to stay in school rather than dropping out to run his business. Unfortunately for Lisa, the founders they meet are Zuckerberg, Bill Gates, and Richard Branson, none of whom completed his degree. The episode aired in October 2010, two days after the release of *The Social Network*.

PHILANTHROPY

Having come from an ordinary background and achieved great things as a result of his own education and the educational background of his parents, Zuckerberg was never going to be a spoiled rich kid. He has worked for his money and understands acutely how much power it gives him. His early charitable donations included an undisclosed sum to Diaspora, an open-source personal web server, and $100 million to the public-school system of Newark, New Jersey. Modest Zuckerberg wanted to make the latter donation anonymous, but New Jersey governor Chris Christie and Newark mayor Cory Booker convinced him to go public.

In 2010, Zuckerberg decided to sign the Giving Pledge, a commitment to give at least 50 percent of his wealth to charity during his lifetime. Other signatories of the pledge include Bill Gates and Warren Buffett. The reasons for spending before you die are numerous and include the ability to decide which projects you support, to leverage your professional network and skills to maximize the positive outcomes of the donations, and to reduce the administration costs associated with having to use a succession of trust vehicles and lawyers to make decisions for you.

> **"The question I ask myself like almost every day is, 'Am I doing the most important thing I could be doing?'"**
>
> —MARK ZUCKERBERG

Since signing the pledge, Zuckerberg has donated 18 million Facebook shares (with a value totaling $990 million) to the Silicon Valley Community Foundation, the largest community foundation in the U.S., which makes grants to domestic and international charities working in community building, economic security, education, immigration, and widening opportunities. He also gave $25 million to help combat the spread of the Ebola virus in 2014.

The Chan Zuckerberg Initiative

Zuckerberg has a daughter, Max, born on December 1, 2015. A week later, Zuckerberg and his wife, Priscilla Chan, marked the occasion by publishing an open letter to their child. They pledged to donate 99 percent of their Facebook shares (valued at the time at around $45 billion) to a new foundation, the Chan Zuckerberg Initiative. The foundation works in health and education, and the money will be spent over the course of Chan's and Zuckerberg's lifetimes.

Technically the Chan Zuckerberg Initiative is neither a private foundation nor a charity; it is a limited liability company. This means it is able to generate a profit, lobby government bodies, and make political donations. This model has drawn some criticism, since the donations Zuckerberg makes to the initiative will be tax deductible. In the words of Michael Miello at *The Daily Beast,* "If purity is the essence here, there seems no reason that the tax system should support it. Zuckerberg can afford to dabble in politics and society without massive subsidies from the rest of the country."

The published mission of the Chan Zuckerberg Initiative is to "advance human potential and promote equality in areas such as health, education, scientific research, and energy." Zuckerberg and Chan intend to take the long view and target their resources for the biggest challenges they expect the next generation to face. The time frame for their work is clear, as in the open letter they wrote: "Medicine has only been a real science for less than 100 years, and we've already seen complete cures for some diseases and good progress for others. As technology accelerates, we have a real shot at preventing, curing, or managing all or most of the rest in the next 100 years."

POLITICAL INVOLVEMENT

Politically, Zuckerberg is a pragmatist. He does not appear to have any particularly strong ideological leanings, and as he has never specified his own political views, observers have placed him in both the conservative and liberal camps. It is likely, and a shrewd business move, that he supports those politicians and parties best able to represent the commercial interests of Facebook and the philanthropic interests of the Chan Zuckerberg Initiative.

That is not to say that Zuckerberg doesn't get involved in politics, however. In February 2013, he hosted his first fund-raising event, for New Jersey governor Chris Christie. Zuckerberg knew Christie from the time of his $100 million donation to Newark's public schools, and later that year he ran a similar fund-raiser for Cory Booker. On both occasions, Zuckerberg's own interest was pushing for education reform, and he believed these two men could help him do it.

In April 2013, Zuckerberg launched a new lobbying group, FWD.us, with three core aims: immigration reform, improving public education, and enabling more technological breakthroughs of benefit to the general public. FWD.us was backed by a number of Silicon Valley entrepreneurs, and its first president was Zuckerberg's friend Joe Green. The group is not aligned with a political party—it favors the bipartisan approach—and though there is some positive evidence of its impact on policy (TechCrunch reported that FWD.us drove 33,500 calls to Congress in summer 2013 and a total of 125,000 actions, including social-media shares), it is less than the founders might have liked. Other criticisms of FWD.us posit that it has a poorly defined long-term agenda and doesn't articulate its vision well.

 Be open about issues that are important to you, and use your platform to advocate for change.

In terms of other politically charged issues he cares about, Zuckerberg has openly supported gay and transgender rights, riding with Facebook's carnival float at the annual San Francisco Lesbian, Gay, Bisexual, and Transgender Pride Celebration in 2013. In the aftermath of the Paris terror attacks in December 2015, he spoke out in support of the Muslim community, explaining that he wanted "to add my voice in support of Muslims in our community and around the world" and reminding others that "as a Jew, my parents taught me that we must stand up against attacks on all communities." Zuckerberg has also voiced his support for the Black Lives Matter campaign, remarking in a memo to staff that "Black Lives Matter doesn't mean other lives don't—it's simply asking that the black community also achieves the justice they deserve." The memo was a response to his discovery that some Facebook employees had crossed out Black Lives Matter graffiti, overwriting it with "All Lives Matter." He was angry about this, on the grounds that the very act of crossing something out "means silencing speech, or that one person's speech is more important than another's."

PERSONAL LIFE

Zuckerberg met his future wife, Priscilla Chan, at a fraternity party in his sophomore year at Harvard, where she was also studying, and the couple started dating in 2003, a year before the birth of Facebook. Chan was born in Braintree, Massachusetts, and grew up just outside Boston as the oldest of three sisters. Her parents were two ethnic-Chinese refugees who arrived in the U.S. on boats of people fleeing Vietnam. In her childhood, she spoke Cantonese at home.

Though quiet and usually in the background, Chan is at least as smart as Zuckerberg. She was her class valedictorian in high school and graduated from Harvard with a BA in biology and a minor in Spanish. After graduating, she taught science for a year, then went on to medical school at the University of

California. She graduated in 2012, married Zuckerberg the same year, and works as a pediatrician. It is likely that Chan is the one who pushed for the health focus in the Chan Zuckerberg Initiative.

 Find a partner, in life as well as in business, who is your equal, intellectually speaking, and shares your values.

Maxima Chan Zuckerberg was long-awaited, as Chan had suffered three previous miscarriages. Zuckerberg had blogged to his 33 million followers about these miscarriages. Although some felt this was oversharing, plenty more were positive about his honesty. He wrote, "We hope that sharing our experience will give more people the same hope we felt and will help more people feel comfortable sharing their stories."

CONCLUSION

Not all of us can be like Mark Zuckerberg, sadly. Intellectually, he is far ahead of most of his Harvard peers, let alone the general public, and his breadth of interests and knowledge is unquestionably unusual too. Only a certain number of companies like Facebook will be founded in any one generation, only one at a time can be *Time* magazine's Person of the Year, and, with $46 billion behind him (and more every passing day), Zuckerberg unquestionably has an advantage. But that is not to say that his personal attributes, his values and interests, and the career path he has chosen cannot be a source of inspiration to us all. There are plenty of lessons we can learn from him and apply in our own lives, which will put us in a stronger position intellectually, personally, financially, and in business.

If we were to summarize the content of this chapter into five unforgettable lessons from Zuckerberg, they would have to be as follows:

1. If you have an idea, develop it. And if it doesn't work out, have another idea, and develop that one, too. Eventually you will come up with an idea you are satisfied with that is commercially viable.

2. When you have found that idea, focus on it. Zuckerberg has focused on Facebook every single day. It's taken a great deal of blood, sweat, and tears, not to mention brainpower, to get this far.

3. Remember that human communication and interaction are the most powerful and emotional channels we have. If you can tap into our need to engage with one another, in a way that is effective but unobtrusive, you have the basis for a successful company.

4. Give back to the society you live and work in. No one succeeds on his or her own, and whether you are at the top of your game or still climbing the ladder, you have a responsibility to contribute your time, money, energy, and ideas to making the world a better place.

5. Even if you live and sleep work, you still need someone in your life to support you when things are tough. Don't overlook your personal life if you want to be truly rich.

Think carefully about what you can do, in each aspect of your life, to apply Zuckerberg's lessons. Your ultimate goal is not just to make money but to be fulfilled and to play a positive role in the world. Mark Zuckerberg is a role model for us all.

Oprah Winfrey

INTRODUCTION

Self-made billionaire Oprah Winfrey has leveraged her public profile to make a $3 billion fortune. She is the richest African American, and greatest black philanthropist, in history. She has honorary doctorates from Duke and Harvard, and in 2013 President Barack Obama awarded her the Presidential Medal of Freedom. Her rise from childhood poverty in rural Mississippi to her teenage years with her single mother in inner-city Milwaukee, including becoming pregnant at 14, is nothing short of a miracle.

What enabled Winfrey to succeed? What are her personal attributes, how does she position herself, and what drives her? Having no material or social advantages in her early life, the lessons she can teach us are invaluable. She is the ultimate role model, an inspiration for people of any race, gender, or social status.

> "Be thankful for what you have; you'll end up having more. If you concentrate on what you don't have, you will never, ever have enough."
>
> —OPRAH WINFREY

CHILDHOOD AND EDUCATION

Oprah Winfrey was born on January 29, 1954, in Kosciusko, Mississippi, to Vernita Lee, an unmarried teenage housemaid, who had conceived her daughter in a one-night stand with a coal miner–turned–barber scarcely older than she was. The child was named Orpah on her birth certificate, a biblical name from the Book of Ruth suggested by her aunt. Her relatives had trouble spelling the name when they wrote it down, and in any case most people who saw it mispronounced it as Oprah. This inadvertent moniker stuck.

Winfrey grew up in desperate poverty. Her mother left the family to look for work shortly after Oprah was born, and the child was cared for by her grandmother, Hattie Mae Lee. The family's situation was such that Winfrey wore dresses made from potato sacks, which marked her as especially bad off even in the poor community where they lived. She was bullied for her appearance by her peers.

 Economic poverty, however desperate, can be overcome.

Young Oprah was smart, however. Her grandmother had already taught her to read by the time Oprah was three years old. She had a good memory and a strong voice, so the congregation at their local church nicknamed her "the Preacher."

Oprah's mother returned when Oprah was six, uprooted her from her grandmother's home, and moved her to Milwaukee, Wisconsin. Vernita Lee worked interminable hours for minimal pay and had little time for her daughter. After giving birth to a second daughter, Patricia, Lee sent Oprah away once again, this time to her biological father, Vernon Winfrey. During Oprah's absence, two more children were born: another daughter, who was put up for adoption for financial reasons, and a son.

As a child, Oprah was molested by her cousin, her uncle, and a family friend. When she attempted to address the abuse with her immediate family years later, they refused to accept what she said, and not until 1986, on one of her own TV shows about sexual abuse, did Winfrey feel able to talk publicly about what had happened to her. The emotional and psychological damage of these years was long-lasting: Winfrey once told a BBC News interviewer that the reason she had chosen not to be a mother was that she herself had not been mothered well.

When she was 13 years old, Winfrey ran away from home and became pregnant at 14; her son was born prematurely and died not long after. Winfrey was just a child herself, with little resources or capacity to care for a baby. After returning to Milwaukee to live with her mother, she attended Lincoln High School and then the more affluent Nicolet High School. She was acutely aware of her poverty and felt her peers were constantly rubbing it in her face. She fell in with a bad crowd and stole money to keep up appearances.

Lee again sent Oprah to live with her father, but this time the arrangement proved more successful. Vernon valued education and made it a priority for Oprah. He sent her to East Nashville Hill School, where she quickly found her feet. She joined the school's speech team and won a prestigious oratory competition; the prize was a full scholarship to study communications at Tennessee State University. Education gave Oprah the springboard she needed to leave Milwaukee, her poverty, and many of her troubles behind.

 Education is the single most important means of creating ambition.

TELEVISION CAREER

While still a university student, Winfrey began putting her communication skills to work. She presented the news part-time at WVOL, a Nashville-based radio station that broadcast predominantly to Tennessee's African American community. After graduation, she moved on to WLAC-TV (a CBS-TV affiliate), also in Nashville, and became its first black female news anchor. Winfrey was also the youngest anchor the channel had ever hired.

 ## Youth need not be a drawback to achievement.

The late 1970s saw Winfrey move through a succession of jobs in local television stations, first to anchor the six o'clock news at WJZ-TV in Baltimore and then to cohost two programs, including the channel's local chat show, *People Are Talking*. Her warmth and enthusiasm engaged viewers, and having a young, dynamic black woman on-screen was a fresh, appealing strategy to the station's executives.

Winfrey's big break—her leap from local broadcasting to a national stage—occurred in 1983, when she was headhunted by WLS-TV in Chicago. She took over its morning talk show, *A.M. Chicago,* and in a matter of months transformed it from a low-performing program to the highest-rated talk show in the city. All eyes were on Oprah to see what she would do next.

 ## You can't sit at home and expect opportunities to pop up.

One of those watching closely was film critic Roger Ebert. He convinced Winfrey to sign a syndication contract with King World, and her morning talk show was renamed *The Oprah Winfrey Show.* Entranced by her intelligence and sass, fans tuned in for an hour every morning, and when the show began national broadcasts, in September 1986, it quickly became the number-one daytime talk show in the United States. In *Time* magazine, journalist Richard Zoglin wrote to the point: "What [Winfrey] lacks in journalistic toughness, she makes up for in plainspoken curiosity, robust humor and, above all, empathy. Guests with sad stories to tell are apt to rouse a tear in Oprah's eye.... They, in turn, often find themselves revealing things they would not imagine telling anyone, much less a national TV audience. It is the talk show as a group-therapy session."

The Oprah Winfrey Show was broadcast nationally from 1986 until 2011, making it one of the longest-running daytime talk shows in history. Initially dismissed as a tabloid show, under Winfrey's direction it became a platform for the host's educational and philanthropic initiatives.

With viewer figures estimated at 20 million a day at the peak of the show's popularity, Winfrey had no shortage of celebrity guests vying for her attention. CBS anchor Gayle King, Oprah's best friend, made a record 141 appearances, and singer Céline Dion totaled 28. Winfrey interviewed such entertainment legends as Tom Cruise, Elizabeth Taylor, and Michael Jackson. Filmed at the singer's home and broadcast live, Jackson's interview was watched by 90 million people, making it the most-watched television interview in history.

But Winfrey wasn't interested in only the rich and famous: She was fascinated by the lives of ordinary people and wanted to bring their experiences to light, prompting discussion among her audiences. She interviewed the parents of murdered children, guests with life-threatening diseases, and victims of abuse. It was during one such interview, with a woman named Trudie Chase in the show's 1989–90 season, that Winfrey broke down on hearing about her guest's history of violent sexual abuse and recounted her own experiences of childhood molestation. Years later, Winfrey invited 200 men who had been victims of abuse as children to appear on an episode of the show's final season, along with director and producer Tyler Perry, himself an abuse survivor, in hopes that it would encourage other victims to realize they did not have to suffer in silence but could be open about what they had endured and try to bring the perpetrators to justice.

> **"The struggle of my life created empathy—I could relate to pain, being abandoned, having people not love me."**
>
> —Oprah Winfrey

Winfrey knew early on that her show was more than just entertainment. By discussing prominent issues in current affairs, such as gun crime, racism, mental illness, and sexual abuse, she could change public attitudes about them. She also knew the show could be a tool for education, so she started one of its most successful endeavors: Oprah's Book Club.

Originally a monthly segment on *The Oprah Winfrey Show,* the book club focused on a book (often a novel) Winfrey had selected to discuss on the air. Four books she featured generated multi-million sales, and they invariably shot straight to the top of the best-seller lists, even if they had originally been published years before. Eckhard Tolle's *A New Earth* sold 3,370,000 copies after being included on the Oprah reading list in 2008. Winfrey combined her book discussions with author interviews and related features, including a visit to the Auschwitz concentration camp with author, Holocaust survivor, and Nobel laureate Elie Wiesel.

In her book *Reading With Oprah: The Book Club That Changed America,* writer and publisher Kathleen Rooney describes Oprah as being "a serious American intellectual who pioneered the use of electronic media, specifically television and the Internet, to take reading—a decidedly non-technological and highly individual act—and highlight its social elements and uses in such a way to motivate millions of erstwhile non-readers to pick up books." *Businessweek* was similarly impressed with the leverage Winfrey had on the publishing industry, claiming, "No one comes close to Oprah's clout: Publishers estimate that her power to sell a book is anywhere from 20 to 100 times that of any other media personality."

Winfrey also used her TV show to encourage audiences to improve their health and well-being and increase their aspirations. Having come from desperate beginnings herself, she knew the importance of role models and believed others could be inspired by her example.

 People in positions of power and influence have a moral responsibility to educate the people who look up to them and to set a positive example.

Although Winfrey's personal opinions held great weight with her television audience, she consistently brought on experts to discuss such matters as health, finance, and marital issues, thus increasing her show's credibility and the status of her guests. The life coach and spiritual teacher Iyanla Vanzant began appearing on the show in the late 1990s, advising mostly on relationship issues; in 2000, *Ebony* magazine named her one of the 100 most influential black Americans. Dr. Phil McGraw, a psychologist from Oklahoma, used his academic background to give advice on relationships, bad habits, bad attitudes, and weight loss; his spin-off show, *Dr. Phil*, debuted in 2002, and in 2014 *Forbes* magazine ranked him the 15th-highest-earning celebrity in the world. Financial expert Suze Orman, who spoke on the show about credit-card debt, budgeting, and other money matters, followed a similarly successful trajectory.

The Oprah Winfrey Show ran until 2011. The 25th season was Winfrey's last, but was it ever impressive: She flew all 300 audience members to Australia, with John Travolta as their pilot; she interviewed President Barack Obama and First Lady Michelle Obama; and the final episode featured appearances by Aretha Franklin, Tom Cruise, Stevie Wonder, Will Smith, and Beyoncé. Hundreds of graduates who had received the Oprah Winfrey Scholarship at Morehouse College were in the audience, and the show received its highest ratings in 17 years.

> **"The greatest discovery of all time is that a person can change his future by merely changing his attitude."**
>
> —Oprah Winfrey

The host's own feelings about this end of an era were frank and generally celebratory. She said to her viewers: "I've been asked many times during this farewell season, 'Is ending the show bittersweet?' Well, I say all sweet, no bitter. And here is why: Many of us have been together for 25 years. We have hooted and hollered together, had our aha! moments; we ugly-cried together, and we did our gratitude journals.... I thank you for tuning in every day, along with your mothers and your sisters and your daughters, your partners, gay and otherwise, your friends and all the husbands who got coaxed into watching *Oprah*. And I thank you for being as much of a sweet inspiration for me as I've tried to be for you."

During the show's lifetime, it received 47 Daytime Emmy Awards, eight GLAAD Media Awards, five Image Awards, and a TV Guide Award. In 2013, *TV Guide* ranked *The Oprah Winfrey Show* as the 19th greatest show of all time.

OTHER MEDIA PROJECTS

B y the mid 1980s, Oprah Winfrey was already a household name, which meant she had her pick of other media projects. She was savvy in her choices, however, always selecting opportunities that furthered her career or related to issues she cared about.

Film

Winfrey made her big-screen acting debut in *The Color Purple* in 1985. Directed by Steven Spielberg, this period drama was an adaptation of the novel of the same name by Alice Walker. Its themes of poverty, racism, and sexism in the American South resonated with audiences, and the film was a box-office success, earning $142 million worldwide. It was also favorably received by critics: the online review site Rotten Tomatoes, which amalgamates critics' reviews, gave the film an overall score of 88 percent, and describes it as "a sentimental tale that reveals great emotional truths in American history." Winfrey appeared in the film as Sofia Johnson, the daughter-in-law of the film's female protagonist, who is herself a victim of sexual abuse but refuses to be cowed by her attackers.

The themes of *The Color Purple* are also evident in some of Winfrey's later films. She appeared as Sethe, a former slave living in Cincinnati in the aftermath of the Civil War, in the 1998 horror-drama *Beloved*; and in 2005, she was executive producer on *Their Eyes Were Watching God,* a television movie based on Zora Neale Hurston's seminal work of African American fiction. Her preparations for her role in *Beloved* were particularly thorough and harrowing: She was tied up, blindfolded and left alone in the woods to have an idea of what it must have been like to be a slave.

Winfrey's film company, Harpo Productions, developed and produced a number of movies and documentaries for HBO, and Winfrey made small appearances, often as a voice-over artist, in animated films. She voiced Gussie the goose in *Charlotte's Web,* Judge Bumbledon in *The Bee Movie,* and Eudora in Disney's *The Princess and the Frog.*

Magazines

Winfrey founded two publications, *O, the Oprah Magazine,* which Fortune declared to be the most successful publishing startup ever, and its spin-off, *O at Home.* First published in 2000, *O* targets primarily middle-aged female readers—the same people who watched Winfrey's TV show. Its namesake appears on every cover, sometimes accompanied by other high-profile women such as Michelle Obama and Ellen DeGeneres; the magazine features advice and inspiration in fashion and beauty, health, finances, and books. Winfrey's image and comments are present throughout.

The paid circulation of *O* peaked in 2004 at 2.7 million copies. Although most magazines experienced declining print sales in the late 2000s, *O* held strong in the marketplace. Today the magazine's circulation hovers around 2.4 million copies, two-thirds of which are sold by subscription, and the rest through newsstands. Its affiliated app gives readers access to videos and the ability to purchase books from Oprah's book list.

 If you are lucky enough to create a product that people want to buy into, be prepared to spin it in different ways.

O at Home, a spin-off of *O, The Oprah Magazine,* was also published by the Hearst Corporation, and after it was launched, in

2004, it quickly grew to have a circulation of 1.4 million. O at Home was published quarterly and focused on home furnishings, decorating tips, and good interior design on a budget. The magazine closed in 2008, as Hearst tried to cut costs in the face of falling ad revenues, and its content themes were reincorporated into O, The Oprah Magazine.

Books

To date, Winfrey has written or cowritten five books on a variety of topics. In 1996, writing with Bill Adler, she released *The Uncommon Wisdom of Oprah Winfrey: A Portrait in Her Own Words.* The book explores the moving story of her early life and rise to fame, along with themes of family, success, weight loss, relationships, and her own struggles, passions, and ambitions. Her views and insight are provided in the form of her inspirational quotations, which Adler elaborates on.

Capitalizing on interest in the self-help field, which itself developed in no small part due to *The Oprah Winfrey Show,* in 1996 Winfrey also cowrote *Make the Connection: 10 Steps to a Better Body and a Better Life* with personal trainer Bob Greene. She is blunt about her own struggles with her weight—she had tried, and failed at, almost every diet imaginable—and the book shows how Greene helped her to lose (and largely keep off) more than 70 pounds by eating more healthfully and exercising regularly to increase her metabolism. Winfrey's own story runs alongside these practical tips, providing encouragement.

Journey to Beloved was published two years later. Written by Winfrey with photographs by Ken Regan, it is the story of how she fell in love with Toni Morrison's Pulitzer Prize–winning novel *Beloved* and decided to make it into a film. The book is principally a production diary, but Winfrey also puts her emotions and vulnerabilities on full display. She is filled with doubts about her ability to play her character, Sethe. Even in the company of so many experienced filmmakers, she worries that she lacks the skill to pull off the project and clearly feels a great weight of responsibility to do justice to Morrison's book and the real people who inspired it.

An excerpt from Winfrey's account: "Tomorrow is the first day of dialogue. Am I ready? I think so. I bring the force and grace of history and pain with me, carrying the Ancestors in my heart, hoping, but also knowing, they, too, carry me.... I ask God for grace, and the power of the spirits whose lives went unnoticed, demeaned and diminished by slavery."

Winfrey's *What I Know For Sure*, published in 2014, collects the best of her columns from *O*, many of which were revised and updated. Candid and moving, uplifting and frequently funny, the essays—on joy, resilience, connection, gratitude, possibility, awe, clarity, and power—provide insight into the author's thoughts and feelings and are intended to help readers define their ambitions, work toward realizing them, and find fulfillment.

Winfrey combines her own experiences with messages for others. For example, "My highest achievement: never shutting down my heart. Even in my darkest moments—through sexual abuse, a pregnancy at 14, lies, and betrayals—I remained faithful, hopeful, and willing to see the best in people, regardless of whether they were showing me their worst. I continued to believe that no matter how hard the climb, there is always a way to let in a sliver of light to illuminate the path forward."

Winfrey held off on publishing a second memoir for many years. Her 2017 memoir, *The Life You Want*, looks at her own life and gives inspirational advice.

Radio

Oprah Radio (originally called Oprah and Friends) was an XM Satellite Radio talk-show channel that operated from 2006 to 2014. Winfrey's first three-year contract was said to be worth

$55 million. Broadcast from her own studio in Chicago, the channel featured not only Winfrey, but also key figures who frequently appeared on her show, such as personal trainer Bob Greene, interior designer Nate Berkus, surgeon and alternative medicine promoter Dr. Mehmet Öz, and spiritual teacher Marianne Williamson.

> **"Think like a queen. A queen is not afraid to fail. Failure is another stepping stone to greatness."**
>
> —OPRAH WINFREY

The topics discussed on Oprah Radio were very similar to those on *The Oprah Winfrey Show*: current affairs, self-improvement, health, nutrition, fitness, relationships, and tips for your home all were featured. The channel was broadcast by a number of companies in succession but ceased broadcasting on December 31, 2014.

Internet

In order to coordinate all her activities and create a hub where fans could access everything in one place, Winfrey launched Oprah.com. According to Quantcast, the website currently receives 4.8 million unique visitors every month (down from 6 million in 2008), 70 percent of whom are in the U.S. The vast majority of visitors to the site are women ages 35 to 65, and by far the largest ethnic group of users is African American. Oprah.com is a mine of well-organized information. The latest stories from *O, The Oprah Magazine,* are on the home page, along with advertisements for courses, events, and branded products available from the O Store, Winfrey's online shop. The home page also includes some video content and an invitation for readers to share their own experiences on a variety of topics, so that they feel engaged.

Engaging your customers and building a sense of rapport with them increases their sense of loyalty to your brand.

The bulk of the website's content is divided into several dozen categories, all of which are accessible from the sidebar menu. These include common topics such as Fashion & Beauty, Food, Health & Wellness, and Inspiration, but also special sections for all of Winfrey's courses, along with television shows produced by the Oprah Winfrey Network. The website has a dedicated discussion area (Community Conversations), an area for competitions and promotions (Sweepstakes), and a bookstore tied in with Oprah's Book Club.

The Books section is one of the most interesting parts of Oprah.com: It is at once a valuable information source promoting Winfrey's educational objectives and also a lucrative moneymaker. Numerous book lists are provided in the Reading Room, and all the titles can be purchased online, generating Oprah.com a referral fee from the vendors.

BUSINESS EMPIRE

Winfrey is acutely aware that she is a multibillion-dollar brand: People want to hear what she has to say, and she can capitalize on this through endorsements and advertising to make megabucks. A single tweet from Winfrey, for example, is thought to have boosted Weight Watchers' earnings by $150 million. Although she is personally shrewd, she has also been very well advised throughout her career, enabling her to make the best business decisions. Unlike many of her wealthy peers, she has not inherited a cent but made her fortune entirely on her own. *Forbes* magazine currently estimates her net wealth at $3.1 billion.

Nicole Aschoff, writing in *The Guardian*, went so far as to describe her as "one of the world's best neoliberal capitalist thinkers." Winfrey embodies the American Dream, although, as Aschoff is at pains to point out, for most people that dream remains simply a fantasy. Economic data do not generally demonstrate upward mobility, yet we still aspire to be like Winfrey. Reality, however brutal, does not blunt our dreams, and a role model like Winfrey—someone who made it against all odds—can make us work harder to try and realize them.

Harpo Productions

Founded in Chicago in 1986, Harpo Productions employs more than 12,000 people and handles the bulk of Winfrey's business empire. (The name Harpo is Oprah spelled backward and is also the name of Winfrey's on-screen husband in *The Color Purple*.) Each of Winfrey's businesses is a subsidiary of Harpo Productions.

Harpo Films, founded in 1993, was once the largest division of Harpo Productions; it developed and produced motion pictures and long-form television programs. Harpo Films had an overlap of interests with Harpo Studios, home of *The Oprah Winfrey Show* in Chicago and where many of her other film and television projects, including *Beloved*, were filmed. Harpo Films closed in 2013.

In addition to producing *The Oprah Winfrey Show*, Harpo Studios also produces *Dr. Phil* (2002–present), *Rachael Ray* (2006–present), *The Dr. Oz Show* (2009–present), and many more. Winfrey's own shows, notably *Oprah Prime*, *Oprah: Where Are They Now?*, *Oprah's Master Class*, and *Oprah's Life Class* are all products of Harpo Studios.

Harpo Print, in partnership with Hearst Publications, publishes *O, The Oprah Magazine*. Harpo Radio was the holding company for Oprah Radio, which broadcast from 2006 to 2014, and Harpo Productions also owns Oprah.com.

The Oprah Winfrey Network

An offshoot of Harpo Productions, the Oprah Winfrey Network (OWN) is also an umbrella for various projects. Founded in 2011, the OWN television channel is available to 82 million households in the U.S., and its content is syndicated internationally. Its ratings—averaging 581,000 in the first quarter of 2015—are reasonable when compared to OWN's competitors but are only a fraction of the 7 million viewers a juicy episode of *The Oprah Winfrey Show* would attract. The network's viewership has been boosted on occasions when a celebrity makes breaking news on a show. Disgraced Tour de France winner Lance Armstrong's public confession that he had used performance-enhancing drugs attracted 4.3 million viewers, and Winfrey's interview with Bobbi Kristina Brown, broadcast on the one-month anniversary of her mother Whitney Houston's death broke that record.

> **"The biggest adventure you can take is to live the life of your dreams."**
>
> —Oprah Winfrey

OWN broadcasts a mix of talk shows and films, both original series and reruns of popular shows, much of it presented in back-to-back episode blocks of the same program. The majority of these are Harpo Studios productions. All of Winfrey's shows are broadcast on the channel, as are those of Nate Berkus, Rachael Ray, and Dr. Phil. Tyler Perry, one of the highest-paid performers in the U.S., signed a contract with OWN in 2012 to produce 90 episodes of original content and broadcast all his new material through the channel. His series, which include *The Haves and the Have Nots* and *Love Thy Neighbor,* have been great successes. Perry's viewer figures now exceed those of Winfrey herself.

AWARDS AND HONORS

In addition to her eponymous talk show's many accolades, Winfrey has received the People's Choice Award for TV news projects four times across three decades (1988, 1997, 1998, and 2004); she was twice nominated for an Academy Award (1986 and 2015); she was given a Lifetime Achievement Award at the Emmys (1998); and in 2005 she was inducted into the NAACP Hall of Fame in recognition of her work in television and film. But Winfrey's awards stretch beyond the world of entertainment: She was honored with the Jefferson Award for Public Service in 1998 and the Peabody Award, also for meritorious public service, in 1995. She received the Bob Hope Humanitarian Award in 2002 and a Kennedy Center Honor in 2010.

One award, however, Winfrey prized above all others. On November 22, 2013, at the White House, President Obama presented her with the Presidential Medal of Freedom, the nation's highest civilian award, which recognizes those who have made "an especially meritorious contribution to the security or national interests of the United States, world peace, cultural or other significant public or private endeavors." As a recipient, Winfrey follows in the footsteps of the Apollo 13 crew, Mother Teresa, and scientist Stephen Hawking.

PHILANTHROPY

Acutely aware of her humble beginnings and the potential her personal wealth has to change lives, Winfrey is an active philanthropist. *Businessweek* reported that she became the first African American to rank among the 50 most generous Americans, and by 2012 she had already given away

$400 million to educational causes alone. She has donated more than 400 scholarships to Morehouse College in Atlanta, Georgia, and in 2013 made a one-off donation of $12 million to develop the Smithsonian's National Museum of African American History and Culture.

Winfrey created Oprah's Angel Network in 1998 to support charitable projects and provide grants to NGOs. She personally covered all administrative costs of the network, so every cent of the $80 million it raised went to the front lines of charities' work. This included a donation of $11 million ($10 million of which was a personal donation from Winfrey) for relief efforts in the wake of Hurricanes Katrina and Rita, which devastated predominantly poor black communities in Texas, Mississippi, Louisiana, and Alabama.

> **"It isn't until you come to a spiritual understanding of who you are—not necessarily a religious feeling, but deep down, the spirit within—that you can begin to take control."**
>
> —Oprah Winfrey

The philanthropic project Winfrey is most proud of, however, is the Oprah Winfrey Leadership Academy for Girls, located near Johannesburg in South Africa. The root of the idea formed in 2000 when Winfrey met with South African president Nelson Mandela. The pair discussed poverty at length and agreed that education was the best way of giving poor South African youths—girls in particular—a chance to improve their lives.

Winfrey initially pledged $10 million for a school and began developing a state-of-the-art campus; her financial commitment increased to $40 million as the scope of the project grew. She began recruiting students in 2006, stipulating that only the brightest but most disadvantaged girls would be accepted. The lavish environment she created for her students drew controversy from multiple quarters, but Winfrey was adamant in its defense, saying, "If you are surrounded by beautiful things and wonderful teachers who inspire you, that beauty brings out the beauty in you."

Today the school has nearly 300 students and is a huge success. In a country where only 14 percent of black girls graduate from high school, these girls buck the trend: Every one of the 72 students in the first graduating class won a place at a university. Graduates frequently go on to study in the U.S., and Winfrey not only pays their tuition but also their living costs, equipping them with everything they need. They call her Mom-Oprah, and she feels very strongly that these girls are her heirs. What they achieve in life will be her proudest legacy.

LEADERSHIP AND INFLUENCE

In 2001, *Time* magazine called Winfrey "arguably the world's most powerful woman." *Life* magazine listed her as the most influential black person of her generation, decreeing her "America's most powerful woman." *Forbes* named her as the world's most powerful celebrity in five different years (2005, 2007, 2008, 2010, and 2013). And even President Obama said that she "may be the most influential woman in the country." Whomever you speak to, at home or abroad, there is no doubt that Winfrey is one of the most influential people on the planet and has been for three decades.

To describe Winfrey's influence on middle America, *The Wall Street Journal* coined the word *oprahfication*. The term has especially been used to refer to speaking out about personal issues and bringing one's private life into the public sphere. Although it was originally used to talk about public confession as a form of therapy, it went on to have applications in the world of politics, encouraging politicians to speak emotionally about their problems and issues of personal importance to them. As *Newsweek* reported, "Every time a politician lets his lip quiver or a cable anchor 'emotes' on TV, they nod to the cult of confession that Winfrey helped create."

Winfrey has deliberately and consistently used her position to influence public opinion on moral and spiritual issues, as well as consumer choices. By providing a safe forum on her talk show and encouraging guests to speak out, she was able to put previously taboo issues on the discussion table in ordinary homes.

Although her critics have accused Winfrey of blurring the lines surrounding "normal" behavior, the general view is that Winfrey just made people understand that differences in sexual preference, for example, exist naturally within any given population and that talking about them is nothing to be ashamed of. As early as 1988, Winfrey invited audience members to stand up and announce their sexuality on air, in observance of National Coming Out Day. She visited a West Virginia town and publicly confronted residents who were paranoid about the presence of a local man with HIV, chastising them for their lack of Christian love. She also invited and actively promoted gay celebrities on her show, and when Ellen DeGeneres announced to the world that she was a lesbian, it was to Winfrey.

Winfrey has guided her fans spiritually, too, both through her own teachings and those of people she has given a platform to on her show. *Christianity Today* described her in an article titled "The Church of O" as "a postmodern priestess—an icon of church-free spirituality." And in the animated comedy series *Futurama,* an episode set 1,000 years from now sees "Oprahism" as a mainstream religion.

Although Winfrey herself is a Christian, she has actively promoted spirituality in all its forms. The American spiritual teacher Gary Zukav, who encourages the alignment of personality with soul to create "authentic power" and transform humanity, was invited to appear on *The Oprah Winfrey Show* on 35 separate occasions, and less than a month after the 9/11 terror attacks, she controversially aired a show called "Islam 101," describing Islam as the "most misunderstood of the three major religions." Rudy Giuliani, then mayor of New York City, asked her to host the Prayer for America service at Yankee Stadium, which she did, and in 2002, President George W. Bush asked her to join a U.S. delegation to Afghanistan. Concerned that it would portray the war on terror in a positive light, however, Winfrey declined the invitation—and the trip was canceled. Without its figurehead, the foremost opinion leader in the country, it was not thought to be worthwhile.

> **"What God intended for you goes far beyond anything you can imagine."**
>
> —OPRAH WINFREY

Winfrey's endorsement in elections is, unsurprisingly, fiercely sought-after. She kept her views on party politics to herself until 2008, when, for the first time, she openly supported a presidential candidate, Barack Obama. Winfrey held a fund-raiser for Obama at her Santa Barbara estate and joined him on the campaign trail in Iowa, New Hampshire, and South Carolina. Economists at the University of Maryland calculated that her endorsement was responsible for between 420,000 and 1,600,000 votes for Obama in the primary alone. Rod Blagojevich, then governor of Illinois, described Winfrey as "the most instrumental person in electing Barack Obama president."

"The Oprah Effect" has as great an impact on consumer purchases as it has on public opinion. According to *The New York Times*, a book recommendation from Winfrey can easily generate 1 million additional sales. But the opposite is also true: If she doesn't like something, and says so publicly, sales fall. During a 1996 program about mad cow disease, for example, Winfrey was horrified by what she heard and said she was "stopped cold from eating another burger." Cattle prices tumbled, allegedly costing beef producers $11 million. Texas cattlemen attempted to sue Winfrey for "false defamation of perishable food" and "business disparagement," but after a two-month trial, she was found not liable for damages.

PERSONAL LIFE

Winfrey has spent the entirety of her adult life as a public figure and has spoken openly about her personal life. The whole concept of Oprahfication is, after all, about making your private life and emotions public as a means of therapy. Winfrey practices what she preaches.

Relationships

Winfrey's romantic life, particularly in her early years, was difficult. After her self-professed promiscuous teenage years, she began to focus on education and pull her life together. She had a number of more meaningful relationships, including, in the late 1970s, dating musician and radio host John Tesh, but according to her biographer, the couple split due to the pressure of a mixed-race relationship.

She also dated a married man who had no intention of leaving his wife. She has talked at length about that relationship and the desperation it made her feel, saying, "The more he rejected me, the more I wanted him. I felt depleted, powerless." When the relationship ended, Winfrey contemplated suicide, even going as far as to write a suicide note. The emotional turmoil led to significant weight gain. Again, Winfrey has spoken frankly about this issue: "I needed everyone to like me, because I didn't like myself much. So I'd end up with these cruel, self-absorbed guys who'd tell me how selfish I was, and I'd say 'Oh, thank you, you're so right' and be grateful to them, because I had no sense that I deserved anything else. Which is also why I gained so much weight later on. It was the perfect way of cushioning myself against the world's disapproval."

 Do not underestimate the emotional impact of a relationship breakdown.

She got together with Stedman Graham in 1986, and although they were engaged to be married in 1992, the couple never actually tied the knot. They are still happily together, unmarried and without children. They prefer to have what they call a "spiritual union."

 It is fine to buck convention in your private and professional lives.

Graham, born in 1951, is a successful businessman and speaker, though his fame and wealth have come about as result of his relationship with Winfrey. He is the author of a dozen self-help books and also writes a column for The Huffington Post.

Winfrey's closest friend is former news anchor Gayle King, whom Winfrey first met in her early 20s. Over the years, some people have suggested that Winfrey and King's relationship was partly sexual in nature, but both women refute this. Writing in the August 2006 issue of *O,* Winfrey said, "There isn't a definition in our culture for this kind of bond between women. So I get why people have to label it—how can you be this close without it being sexual?... I've told nearly everything there is to tell. All my stuff is out there. People think I'd be so ashamed of being gay that I wouldn't admit it? Oh, please."

 Your friends have helped to make you the person you are today. Celebrate your friendship and support one another.

Winfrey considers the writer Maya Angelou to be both a friend and a mentor, referring to the older woman as "mother-sister-friend." When Angelou turned 70 in 1998, Winfrey arranged a weeklong cruise for Angelou and 150 of her guests; a decade later, she hosted a similarly lavish affair at Donald Trump's Mar-a-Lago club in Palm Beach, Florida.

CONCLUSION

Winfrey has said, "I don't think of myself as a poor, deprived ghetto girl who made good. I think of myself as somebody who, from an early age, knew I was responsible for myself, and I had to make good." Regardless of how Winfrey feels about herself, she is, for more than a generation of people—African American women in particular—the ultimate role model, a woman who has made it despite seeming to have all of life's odds stacked against her. Her story is one of hope, and perhaps more than anyone else in the country, Winfrey embodies the American Dream. But she indisputably made that dream come true for herself. She didn't inherit her money, marry into it, or receive any other notable handouts. She has earned every cent through legitimate business interests: There is not even a hint of scandal or wrongdoing in her past; that in itself is remarkable for someone of her wealth.

> **"I still have my feet on the ground. I just wear better shoes."**
>
> —OPRAH WINFREY

Some lessons from Winfrey's life come through stronger than others, and though the chances of any of us following exactly in her footsteps are slight, by implementing these lessons in our own lives, we can certainly improve our lot.

First of all, education is the single most effective way of lifting people out of poverty. If you cannot access education, you cannot hope to advance. Winfrey understands from personal experience just what a difference a good education can make to aspiration and lifetime achievement; this is why she invests so much of her time, money, and effort into educational initiatives.

Second, no one else is going to do it for you. If you are fortunate, there will be other people around you to encourage, support, and teach you and give you a lucky break. But it's up to you to position yourself in such a way that you are able to take full advantage of them, remain focused, and work hard consistently.

Third, and perhaps most important, you must have credibility. If you are the face of your brand, your customers will not differentiate between what you do and what your company does. If you are providing advice, it must be of the highest quality, and you should get input from experts. If you are creating a product, it must be something others want to buy and can believe in. You cannot do one thing and say something else. You must be open about your shortcomings and the things you have gotten wrong. Be prepared to accept criticism and to learn from it. Show others that you are still human, and they will respect you all the more for it.

Richard Branson

INTRODUCTION

Richard Branson is possibly the world's most famous businessman. From Australia to Zimbabwe, Atlanta to Zagreb, and everywhere in between, the Englishman and his infamous publicity stunts get people talking. Even if you cannot name a single one of his more than 400 companies, you will recognize this laid-back celebrity with the goatee and the cheeky grin. Branson is a master of self-promotion, and the column inches he personally generates are a major contributing factor to his Virgin Group's success. He was knighted by Prince Charles at Buckingham Palace in March 2000 for his services to entrepreneurship, and in 2014 *The Sunday Times* voted him the most admired businessperson in the past five decades. Just how did he manage to get there?

"Screw it, let's do it!" is Branson's motto, and it has become so closely associated with him that it even inspired the title of his 2011 book, *Screw Business as Usual*. Branson is known for his direct approach to everything he does. He is a mischievous chap who gets to the point without bothering with airs and graces, and he treads frequently and knowingly on the toes of the establishment. When he sees something he wants, personally or commercially, he grabs it with both hands. Every now and then, this ballsy approach pays off spectacularly.

In 1979, for example, Branson first saw a beautiful island called Necker in the British Virgin Islands. The asking price was $6 million, but when he scraped together absolutely every penny he had, it totaled only $100,000. Rather than fearing what might happen, he put all his cash on the table, and the estate agents immediately laughed him out of the room. A year later, they came back groveling. No one else had put in a bid for Necker, and the sellers wanted Branson's money after all. He bought his $6 million island for just $100,000 in cash. Today, it's worth somewhere in the region of $200 million; it is the party island of choice for the world's celebrities, from Kate Winslet to Prince Harry; and it is quite possibly the best investment Branson ever made. It was an impulse buy with no commercial basis, but he followed his gut, invested in something he wanted and knew he would enjoy, and his passion and good fortune combined to make it a success. Branson now lives on Necker for much of the year, and he wouldn't part with it for the world. Let's learn from this example.

EARLY YEARS

Richard Charles Nicholas Branson was born on July 18, 1950, and is the eldest of three children. His father, Edward, was a barrister, respected and comfortably wealthy but by no means a society figure, despite his own father, Richard's grandfather, being a titled high-court judge. Richard's mother, Eve, had been a professional ballet dancer and a flight attendant prior to her marriage. A stay-at-home mom, she supplemented the family income with small entrepreneurial projects, including producing craft items to sell; Richard and his two sisters were encouraged to help their mother make them. The family was always close, and right from the start Richard had a particularly strong relationship with his mother.

The Branson siblings grew up in the south of England, where they enjoyed an idyllic childhood, though discipline at home was strict. In his biography, Branson describes how, when he was five years old, his mother kicked him out of the family car three miles from home and told him to walk the rest of the way. It was his punishment for causing a disturbance in the back seat. He saw this as a turning point in his childhood: For the first time, he had to take responsibility for his actions, and he was forced to overcome his innate shyness and talk to strangers in order to get home. It was a lesson that would stand him in good stead in later life.

Schooling was a trial for Branson, and he probably didn't get a great deal out of the experience, at least not academically. He was privately educated, first at Scaitcliffe School, a prep school in Surrey, and then at the independent Stowe School in Buckinghamshire. He suffered, then as now, from dyslexia, which was neither diagnosed nor supported, and he performed poorly on exams and coursework. Though a popular and lively student, he was often disruptive, and on Branson's final day at school, his headmaster, Robert Drayson, foretold that young Richard would either end up in prison or become a millionaire. Branson has done both, though you can add a few extra zeroes to those millions.

GETTING INTO BUSINESS

Fresh out of school and with no commercial experience or qualifications, 17-year-old Branson founded *The Student* magazine, which would become the first brick in the Virgin empire. It was 1968, and Branson recognized early on the significant consumer power of young people and how their interests differed substantially from those of their parents. The magazine was timely, and it capitalized on fashions and moods in universities and colleges across the United Kingdom. The inaugural issue featured insightful interviews with prominent celebrities such as the actress Vanessa Redgrave and artist David Hockney; there was a short story by John Le Carré, as well as inspiring feature articles on white slavery and the resistance to the Vietnam War. All the content was designed to encourage discussion among readers and their friends.

Right from this first step, Branson had his eye on the bottom line. Interviewing celebrities and publishing magazines was fun, but financially it still had to break even. Making calls from phone booths, young Branson recruited advertisers who paid for their products to appear in the magazine. He gave them the opportunity to promote their goods in front of a very specific group of consumers, and they recognized the value of this. These sums were small, but they were a start.

With *The Student* up and running, Branson realized that not only could he advertise other people's products, but he had a ready-made platform for selling his own, too. What's more, he wouldn't have to pay anyone else to advertise them. He opened his own shop, Virgin Records and Tapes, with his friend Nik Powell in Notting Hill in 1971, selling vinyl records over the counter and by mail order.

Branson advertised the records and the bands in his magazine and substantially undercut the prices of his mainstream competitors. The name Virgin was suggested by one of Branson's first employees. Although it was a bit risqué, it referred principally to the fact that they were all new to business and had little idea what to expect or do.

Branson and Powell didn't sell just any records: They chose the coolest artists of the day and specialized in so-called krautrock (German electronic music, a particular favorite of BBC Radio 1 DJ John Peel) and progressive rock. Both styles were on the cusp of reaching the big time and appealed to Virgin's student market. Hanging out at the shop became half of the appeal for customers; you could meet with friends, sit on the beanbag chairs, and tuck into vegetarian snacks. The entire shopping experience was new, so even without the low prices, customers would still have come to Virgin over other record stores, because it was the place to see and be seen.

We can already see aspects of Branson's modus operandi emerging by the early 1970s. The characteristics of these two early businesses didn't guarantee their overnight success or even their long-term survival, but they were key factors in Branson's later commercial endeavors.

The Virgin brand has been at the heart of Branson's businesses from these early days. It certainly catches people's attention, and they remember it. It wins by virtue of its association with sex but is not in itself something overtly sexual or offensive. If anything, it falls in the great British tradition of innuendo and makes people smile. By promoting his diverse range of products under the single Virgin umbrella, Branson capitalizes on brand familiarity and respect. If people recognize the name Virgin, be it in the context of mobile phones, airlines, cosmetics, or records, they immediately associate the product with Branson and expect it to be affordable, fun, and well done.

 Choose your name with care. It can make all the difference.

Branson understood right from the start that a company needn't exist in isolation, and indeed it can be mutually beneficial if two companies work together. *The Student* gave Branson's record store a boost, and later he used the market knowledge he gained through both of these businesses to build Virgin Records. The same pattern is evident throughout his career: Why sell just airline tickets when you can use your knowledge and customer base to sell vacations and even space travel?

 Create brands with overlapping interests.

Branson always aims to be ahead of the curve. He does his market research and acts on his hunches about the next big thing. This enables him to have the first-mover advantage over his competitors and means that customers always see Virgin at the cutting edge of innovation. Branson identified brands and musical styles and marketed them to the public just as they were becoming popular, riding on the back of their growth. Likewise, he made sure that Virgin planes were the first to be equipped with in-flight Wi-Fi, anticipating customer demand, and founded Virgin Galactic back in 2004, long before space tourism would become a reality.

 Choose fashionable products to sell.

Customer service and the customer experience set Virgin apart. With Virgin Records and Tapes, we see Branson's desire and ability to create an environment that customers loved; it was not just a shop but a place to meet, eat, and share ideas. No one else had thought to sell records this way, and that put Virgin at a distinct advantage. Customers have always come first for Branson. As he has put it, "Simplicity and good customer service will win every time." He still calls a random selection of customers personally to ask for their feedback and makes his personal phone number and email address available so people can always come to him with ideas and criticism.

 Put the customer's experience first.

Branson's rise to power was not smooth, however. One particular event in his early career could well have stopped the Virgin empire in its tracks. By the end of 1971, Virgin Records and Tapes had added a shop in Oxford Street. It was caught selling vinyl records that had been declared as export stock—i.e., no tax had been paid when Branson purchased them. Although this enabled him to keep prices low and increase his sales margins, it was a criminal offense and one that British Revenue & Customs and the

London Metropolitan Police took very seriously. Branson spent a night in jail, he had to pay all of the unpaid taxes, and he was heavily fined.

Most small businesses would have folded at this stage; there was no way to pay the fine and the back taxes, either from his savings or from future profits. It was Branson's mother who stepped in to save the day. She remortgaged the family home to help pay the settlement, so Branson could continue the business. He was heavily indebted to her for her generosity. Forty years on, Branson is still close to his mother (his father died in 2011), and his children, Holly and Sam, are equally important public brand ambassadors for Virgin, though they have their own independent careers.

 Your family are your greatest supporters and an asset to your business, but don't take advantage of them.

As Branson found, bending the rules can help you get rich quick, but in the long term it will come back to bite you. Knowing the rules and regulations and complying with them has meant that Virgin and Branson himself are respected around the world and that he has largely avoided the damaging tax scandals that have damaged the public reputation of companies like Google, Starbucks, and Vodafone.

 Keep on the right side of the law.

If Branson's mother hadn't stepped into the breach, Virgin would have died a premature death. Branson understands from personal experience that "In business, protecting against the downside is critical." You have to plan for the rainy day and make sure that there is money in the pot to cover all eventualities, even ones you don't expect. Think of it as an insurance policy.

 Cash flow (or lack thereof) can kill small companies.

THE RISE OF VIRGIN

Branson recovered from this setback and used Virgin Records and Tapes as the springboard for his next project, the business that would change his life forever. He launched the Virgin record label in 1972 with his existing business partner and two other men, Simon Draper and Tom Newman. Time spent in the record shop interacting with his customers meant Branson had done his market research thoroughly and had a fair idea about what his future customers would want to buy. Interviews he had conducted for *The Student* gave him a ready-made network of musicians, DJs, and agents to work with, and this again gave him a fighting chance in the label's early days.

Luck was on Virgin Records' side. The first artist to sign was multi-instrumentalist Mike Oldfield, and Virgin sealed the deal by offering him a free session in its recording studio, the Manor Studio, which was inside Branson's Oxfordshire home. The resulting progressive-rock album Oldfield recorded and Virgin released was *Tubular Bells*. It has sold more than 15 million copies worldwide (including nearly 3 million in the U.K.), stayed on the charts for 279 weeks, and was even played during the opening ceremony of the 2012 London Olympics. Several more chart successes followed, including the electronic album *Phaedra* and *The Faust Tapes.*

Branson had two priorities: getting the right artists and selling records at the right price. He famously sold the *Faust* album for 49 pence, typically the price of a vinyl single. To students with limited budgets, the choice was obvious. Why would you buy one track on vinyl when you could have a whole album from Virgin Records on tape?

Virgin Records was gaining traction but principally recorded and distributed music by new or little-known artists. That would all change in 1977 when Branson signed the Sex Pistols. The band had previously recorded on both the EMI and A&M labels, but the members' erratic behavior and frequent scandals made them unreliable and they were dropped, considered by management to be too much of a liability. Branson saw his ·opportunity, and Virgin Records stepped into the vacuum. This decision catapulted the record company into the mainstream. Some of the most important progressive-rock artists of the late 1970s and early '80s now clamored to join Virgin Records, including Culture Club and the Human League, whose single "Don't You Want Me" went straight to No. 1 on the U.K. singles charts in 1981.

> **"Screw it, let's do it!"**
>
> —RICHARD BRANSON

Yet again realizing the potential of cross-pollinating his businesses, Branson purchased the gay nightclub Heaven, a superclub beneath London's Charing Cross Station. Not afraid of courting controversy (gay clubs were still relatively unknown at the time) he promoted his artists and DJs through the club, widening the appeal of his records and using the column inches generated about Heaven to raise the profile of Virgin Records.

For the first time, Branson was making money, and lots of it. He bought the Kensington Roof Gardens in 1981 and in quick succession founded Virgin Vision (later Virgin Communications), Virgin Games, Virgin Atlantic Airways, Virgin Holidays, and British Satellite Broadcasting (BSB, a joint venture with Anglia, Granada, and Pearson). He was no longer thinking just about the London or U.K. market but building a global brand with a strong footprint in the U.S. as well as Europe.

It is beyond the scope of this chapter to look at all his companies in detail, but the early days of Virgin Atlantic Airlines (founded in 1984) are particularly worthy of note. Virgin Atlantic had its roots in another airline, formed the year before as British Atlantic Airways (BAA) to operate flights between the U.K., the U.S., and the Falkland Islands, where a war between Argentina and Britain had just ended. Branson met one of BAA's founders, American Randolph Fields, at a friend's party in London, and after lengthy negotiations, Branson came on board as a business partner. The airline was renamed Virgin Atlantic, and shortly afterward, Branson bought out Fields for a lump sum of £1 million and a further payment from the airline's first dividend.

> **"Business opportunities are like buses. There's always another one coming."**
>
> —RICHARD BRANSON

Branson wasn't actually looking for an airline to buy; he was looking for an opportunity, and when one came along, he seized it. In the 1980s, British Airways (Virgin Atlantic's main competitor) was the only U.K. airline operating long-haul routes. British Airways' customer service was known to be poor, so Branson quickly realized he could attract customers not by slicing fares but by offering more comfortable planes and superior service during the booking process and in flight. Virgin Atlantic at first was restricted to operating flights only out of Gatwick but in 1991 was granted permission to fly from Heathrow, too, much to British Airways' chagrin.

Virgin Atlantic got off to a fairly strong start because Branson identified a genuine customer demand and made sure his new airline filled it. It was not smooth sailing, however, and the company experienced financial difficulties throughout the early 1990s. In spite of his deep fondness for Virgin Records, Branson sold the brand to EMI in 1992 for approximately £560 million and used the proceeds to shore up his airline's finances. This was a hard decision—Branson cried when the deal was done—but he knew the importance of prioritizing financial stability and long-term returns above personal attachment to an individual product or brand. The gamble paid off, and Branson and Virgin Atlantic both lived to fight another day, but they were not yet out of trouble.

Throughout the 1990s, British Airways ran a publicity campaign against Virgin Atlantic, nicknamed the "Dirty Tricks" campaign. British Airways objected to Branson's publicity stunts and attacked him personally just as viciously as it attacked the airline in a bid to put the company out of business. The plan backfired: Branson sued British Airways for libel and won. The airline had to pay a legal bill of £3 million, personal damages of £500,000 to Branson, and a further £110,000 to Virgin Atlantic. If anything, the failed British Airways campaign actually improved Virgin's standing with the public, as people enthusiastically backed David against Goliath and were elated when David won.

Today Virgin Atlantic has an annual turnover of £2.87 billion, employs around 10,000 people, and carries 5.5 million passengers on international flights each year. It is one of the largest and best-known brands in Branson's Virgin Group and a major trendsetter in the global airline market.

MANAGING 400 COMPANIES

The Virgin Group is a global success story. The group employs 50,000 people worldwide and in 2012 had total revenues in excess of $24 billion. According to the *Forbes* 2014 Rich List, Branson personally was worth nearly $5 billion, making him the seventh richest person in the U.K. How has he made this money, and how does he manage such success? Let's look at three Virgin case studies, three successful businesses Branson has grown and operated in quite different ways, and then some of the more unusual but personally rewarding projects he has launched using the money and profile he generated through his more conventional platforms.

Virgin Media

Founded in 2006, with headquarters in New York and the U.K., Virgin Media offered digital television, broadband internet, and fixed-line and mobile telephone services, making it the first "quadruple play" network in the U.K. The company's revenue in 2012 was £4.1 billion, and total assets were in excess of £10.5 billion. It was one of the Virgin Group's flagship companies, but Branson sold it to Liberty Global for £15 billion in 2013. This makes it a particularly interesting case study.

In 1999, Branson founded Virgin Mobile U.K., the world's first mobile virtual network operator. Two other companies, NTL and Telewest, merged in 2006 and four months later bought Virgin Mobile for £962.4 million in cash and shares, giving Branson a 10.1 percent stake in the new company. He rebranded it as Virgin Media, licensing the Virgin name for a 30-year period because he recognized its importance to the company's long-term success.

Virgin Media was an innovative company in many ways. It owned and operated its own fiberoptic cable network, the only nationwide cable network in the U.K.; it launched Virgin Central, one of the first on-demand TV services; and in 2009 and 2010 the company came out on top in Ofcom's broadband speed tests, showing that its investment in infrastructure was paying off. The company experimented with various ways of streaming content and in 2012 won an exclusive contract to provide Wi-Fi on the London Underground network until 2017.

Why then, if Virgin Media had first-rate products and was making money, did Branson sell it? It comes down to leverage. Branson only ever had a 10.1 percent stake in Virgin Media. In 2007 Branson hedged 37 percent of this stake for a $224 million loan, and when the repayment came due, he decided not to buy back the 12.8 million mortgaged shares. Instead, he reinvested the money in other Virgin Group projects, including the Virgin Green Fund (for investments in the renewable-energy and energy-efficiency sectors). The decision to sell Virgin Media was therefore not Branson's alone; he was only the company's third-largest shareholder, and the shareholders collectively approved the sale. Branson's personal feelings, if indeed he did oppose the deal, were overshadowed by the views of the majority.

Branson made money from Virgin Media and has used the profits to diversify his portfolio, which is an admirable strategy. He stayed with Virgin Media through its most rapid period of growth, then sold out before competitors caught up and ate into its profits.

Virgin Atlantic

When consumers think of Branson and airlines, they think of Virgin Atlantic, but in fact, the Virgin Group operates a number of airlines, all separate legal entities. These have included Virgin America, Virgin Australia, Virgin Samoa, Virgin Nigeria, and Virgin Express. The strength of this model is that if any one airline fails, it does not automatically endanger the survival of the others: Virgin Nigeria, for example, could simply be cut off; its losses did not have a detrimental impact on other parts of the company.

Virgin Atlantic is headquartered in Crawley, England, and shares offices with Virgin Holidays. The physical and legal proximity of the two brands is important because it enables them to have a symbiotic relationship: Just as Branson used *The Student* to sell records in his shop, and his music industry network to sign artists to the Virgin label, so too can he up-sell and cross-sell products from the airline to the travel agency and vice versa. He has, in essence, created a one-stop shop for consumers planning their vacations, and thus he can make an enviable profit on every part of the holiday package.

> **"The art of delegation is absolutely key."**
>
> —RICHARD BRANSON

In 2009, Virgin Atlantic made £68.4 million in pretax profits despite the recession and rising oil prices. British Airways lost £401 million in the same period. How did Branson beat the odds? First, Virgin Atlantic carried 5.8 million passengers in 2009, a large proportion of them in premium classes, increasing its profit margin on sales. The company had also planned ahead by prepurchasing fuel, so when oil prices soared, it didn't have to pay them. Virgin Atlantic's fuel bill that year was only £1 billion, a third of British Airways'. Since 2009, Virgin Atlantic hasn't been so lucky, and in the financial year 2012 to 2013, it suffered record losses in the region of £135 million. Cutting costs and increasing profits on long-haul flights became the two greatest priorities, and some critics wondered if Branson would be able to turn around Virgin Atlantic's fortunes at all.

Branson managed to halve Virgin Atlantic's losses in 2013 and expected to return to profitability by 2015. Virgin Atlantic's turnover and load factor (the percentage by which an aircraft is filled) increased. The relationship with Delta Airlines, which bought into Virgin Atlantic in 2013, has also widened the appeal of the airline in the U.S. market by opening up 84 new destinations in the States. New uniforms designed by Vivienne Westwood generated press coverage and made the airline seem far more glamorous than its competitors, and the arrival of 16 brand-new Boeing 787-9 Dreamliners meant Virgin Atlantic's long-haul routes were even more comfortable than before.

None of these changes was dramatic, but Branson is good at looking at the bigger picture and then working back to identify the many little steps required to make an impact overall. The parts of Virgin Atlantic that are not viable in the long-term will be cut off, while those with commercial potential will be strengthened with the funds released from elsewhere, and in this way, Virgin Atlantic will remain a fixture in our skies for many years to come.

Virgin Trains

One of the major brands the Virgin Group operates in the U.K. is Virgin Trains, a company Branson founded in 1997. His goal was to substantially increase the speed of journeys and the quality of customer service after the notoriously inefficient British Rail was privatized. He invested heavily in upgrading lines and purchasing new rolling stock, enabling trains to run at 125 mph on some routes. Operating railway services in the U.K. is highly capital-intensive and risky, as you have to invest in infrastructure with no guarantee that your franchise will be renewed. Branson was hit in exactly this way when he lost part of his franchise to another company.

The costs were offset in part by taxpayer subsidies, and though these kept Virgin Trains running, some critics have attacked the company's dependence on them. These critics believe Branson's modus operandi is to identify industries with little competition, benefit from taxpayer subsidies, and then cash out, profiting from the taxpayers' hard-earned cash. Branson does sometimes profit from taxpayer subsidies, but on those occasions when rail fares and government subsidies do not equal the train operator's running costs, Virgin Trains is in effect subsidizing the rail service.

Dream Projects

The last category of Branson's many projects includes those that are not yet viable but at one stage might well be. Perhaps the most ambitious of these is Virgin Galactic, a commercial space-flight company. Branson founded Virgin Galactic in 2004 with the intention of offering suborbital flights to space tourists. He anticipated the first flight would happen in 2009, but a number of setbacks kept his dream from becoming reality. He does, however, remain optimistic. The Virgin Group initially invested $100 million into Virgin Galactic, followed by $380 million from the sovereign wealth fund of Abu Dhabi and $200 million from the New Mexico state government. NASA has invested a relatively small sum of $4.5 million for research. When you dream big, it seems, other people will dream big too.

So far, it is hard to establish when and how the investors expect to get their money back. As of 2013, 640 potential space tourists have signed up, each paying $200,000. This $12.8 million is a fraction of what has been invested, and though investors argue that the price of space travel will come down, Virgin Galactic tickets have already increased in price, to $250,000. The fourth test flight of a Virgin Galactic spacecraft, the VSS *Enterprise*, ended in disaster in October 2014 when it broke apart in midair and crashed into the Mojave Desert, killing test pilot Michael Alsbury and seriously injuring his copilot, Peter Siebold.

Although Branson started out in space tourism early, the decade of delays meant that he lost his head start. Three other companies, the Sierra Nevada Corporation, XCOR Aerospace, and SpaceX (see the chapter on Elon Musk in this book) are now all developing their own reusable crewed suborbital and orbital spaceplanes. SpaceX was awarded a $2.6 billion contract from NASA, and as the company was already trying to schedule a crewed flight for 2016, it is likely that it, not Virgin Galactic, will become the first private company to successfully launch humans into space.

> **"I sometimes think in life you've got to dream big by setting yourself seemingly impossible challenges.... If you don't dream, nothing happens. And we like to dream big."**
>
> —RICHARD BRANSON

Branson may have more success with Virgin Green, the venture-capital firm he established to invest in renewable and efficient energy sources in Europe and the U.S. It will enable Branson to spread risk across a large number of projects and to cherry-pick the best ideas and teams. Some of the companies Virgin Green Fund has invested in include Gevo, Inc., a biofuels company that converts renewable raw materials into hydrocarbons and isobutanol; Quench, an ultraviolet-water-filtration company; and Metrolight, a provider of electronic ballast solutions for high-intensity discharge lighting systems. Not all the investments will come to fruition: Solyndra, a California company that manufactured solar cells, looked initially to be a good investment but collapsed in 2011 because it could not compete with conventional solar panels.

As far as personal projects go, everyone needs a hobby, and if you have a fortune at your disposal, you can afford to have an expensive hobby. In Branson's case, that hobby is hot-air ballooning. Branson laid out a set of challenges for himself, a series of balloon journeys no one had accomplished before. He broke the distance record for a hot-air balloon in 1987, when he crossed the Atlantic, reaching speeds of 142 mph. Four years later, he crossed the Pacific and set a new record of 245 mph. But the biggest challenge remained: Branson wanted to be the first person to circumnavigate the globe by balloon. He attempted this twice, in 1995 and 1998, but was ultimately beaten to the record by the crew of the Breitling Orbiter 3 later in 1998. Branson took his defeat gracefully and turned his attention to a number of other record-breaking feats, including the fastest crossing of the English Channel in an amphibious vehicle (1 hour, 40 minutes, and 6 seconds in March 2004).

HUMANITARIAN WORK

One of the most interesting of Branson's personal projects is the Elders, a dedicated group of leaders who work together to solve global conflicts. The idea for the group came out of a series of discussions Branson had with South African president Nelson Mandela and the musician Peter Gabriel in the early 1990s, and it was announced formally in 2007 in a speech Mandela gave on the occasion of his 89th birthday. Former UN Secretary General and Nobel Peace Prize winner Kofi Annan chairs the group, and other high-profile members include Gro Harlem Brundtland (former prime minister of Norway), Martti Ahtisaari (former president of Finland, Nobel Peace Prize winner, and the UN's Special Envoy to Kosovo), and former president Jimmy Carter. During his lifetime, Mandela was an honorary Elder, as was Desmond Tutu. Branson is not an Elder himself, but along with Gabriel he uses his money to fund their work and to raise the profile of issues they are trying to resolve.

Branson also uses his money and influence to support the International Centre for Missing & Exploited Children and the

Branson School of Entrepreneurship, which aims to improve economic growth and stability in South Africa. He has backed the Global Zero campaign to eliminate nuclear weapons and has spoken out on a wide range of issues, from calling Uganda to account for its anti-homosexuality legislation to increasing public awareness about wildlife poaching and trafficking. Although he does maintain an interest in the running of the Virgin Group, he has delegated the day-to-day affairs and now concentrates his efforts primarily on humanitarian projects.

> "In a company's first year, your goal should be simply to survive, and this will likely take everything you've got. No matter how tired or afraid you are, you have to figure out how to keep going."
>
> —RICHARD BRANSON

FAILURE AND CRITICISM

Not everything Branson touches works out as he'd like it to, as he is first to admit, and even his ultimately profitable companies often struggled financially in their first few years. Branson's message to his disciples is clear: If you can get over this initial hurdle, you have at least a chance of long-term success.

There is, however, an argument that says to be a good businessperson you also have to know when to quit. It doesn't matter how good a business idea looks on paper; there are always numerous reasons it may not work in practice, and you have to be able to look critically at your product, what is going wrong, and whether it is both feasible and cost-effective to rectify the problems. The case studies of Branson's failures contain valuable lessons for us all.

 Persistence and optimism pay off. Motivate yourself to keep going but know when to walk away.

Virgin Cola

Perhaps the most well-publicized failure of a Virgin brand was that of Virgin Cola, which Branson founded in 1994. He believed he could go head-to-head with the two biggest soft-drinks brands in the world, Coca-Cola and Pepsi, whom he dubbed the "cola duopolists." The product launch was public-relations gold: Branson drove a vintage Sherman tank through New York's Times Square, crushing Coca-Cola bottles under its tracks before opening fire on a Coca-Cola billboard. He erected a 40-foot Virgin Cola billboard above the Times Square Virgin Megastore; the drink's bottle was shaped to resemble actress and pinup Pamela Anderson's voluptuous curves. Branson also paid a fortune to the makers of the hit TV show *Friends* to ensure the sitcom's characters were seen drinking Virgin Cola in the episodes.

Branson soon disagreed over the business development strategy with his partner, Canadian drinks manufacturer Cott Corporation, which owned a 50 percent stake in Virgin Cola. Branson bought Cott out to go it alone in the U.S. market, while in the U.K. he partnered with two relatively small drinks companies, neither of which had much marketplace clout. The serious pitfall, however, was that Branson underestimated the strength of Coca-Cola's and Pepsi's market domination, particularly where brand recognition and distribution networks were concerned. Branson freely admits, "We often move into areas where the customer has traditionally received a poor deal and where the competition is complacent," but Virgin Cola was a case in which this did not apply. Customers were happy with the existing products, and Coca-Cola and Pepsi were far from complacent when dealing with new competitors snapping at their heels. Coca-Cola's immediate response to Virgin Cola's appearance was to double its advertising and promotion budget overnight, drowning out Virgin's publicity.

By 1999, Virgin Cola had captured only 3 percent of the U.K. cola market and never made a penny in profit. This was largely due to distribution difficulties: Most restaurant chains, cinemas, and bars already had exclusive long-term distribution contracts with either Coca-Cola or Pepsi that they were unable or unwilling to break, even if Virgin Cola was more competitively priced. By the early 2000s, even the major supermarket chains had stopped stocking the brand, and the last stockist dropped it in 2009, stating that it would no longer give Virgin Cola shelf space when competitors sold far better. Branson reflected, "That business taught me not to underestimate the power of the world's leading soft-drink makers. I'll never again make the mistake of thinking that all large, dominant companies are sleepy!"

 Humility can be just as important as confidence.

With Branson, though, even bleak situations seem to have an unexpected silver lining. Virgin Cola continued to be sold profitably under license in Nigeria and the Philippines, two markets where the Virgin Group would not otherwise have a prominent presence, and as Branson proclaimed proudly, "We're still number one in Bangladesh!" This may not have been what he set out to achieve, but at least he is able to think positively.

Virgin Brides and Virgin Vie

Another of Branson's failures was Virgin Brides, which Branson launched in 1996, publicizing it in his own inimitable style by shaving off his beard and donning a lacy white wedding dress and veil. When the company closed its last bridal-wear store, in 2007, Branson joked to reporters, "Why did Virgin Brides fail? Because we soon realized there weren't any!" Branson's critics suggested the promo shots of Branson in drag may well have been an own goal as well. The reality is more likely that, as with soft drinks, the wedding gowns and accessories market was already saturated, and a gimmicky change of stores simply didn't appeal to the target consumer.

The third Branson failure we're going to examine is Virgin Vie, which was founded as the Virgin Cosmetics Company in 1997; Branson gave the owners financial backing and allowed them to operate under the Virgin umbrella. It was expected that Virgin Vie would open 100 stores within five years, but the brand struggled to gain traction. It was rebranded as Virgin Cosmetics in 1999, as a way to make its offerings more obvious, but because the range included not only skincare products and makeup but also aromatherapy oils, jewelry, and housewares, the brand was a bit of a mishmash. Virgin Vie signed a partnership agreement with an Asian company in 2001 in a bid to open up international markets. The following year it had 7,000 distributors, mostly in China, Southeast Asia, and South Africa, but the company was overstretched and was forced to close all its stores quite suddenly in 2003.

The company limped on through the 2000s until there was a management buyout in 2009. Virgin had to pay £8.8 million to extract the Virgin name and wrote off an estimated £21 million in loans. Branson had little involvement in the firm. It was not his idea, he had not researched the market, and though he funded the enterprise, neither he nor his core team were involved on a day-to-day basis. The Virgin magic is about the ideas, the team, and the drive behind Virgin products, not only the name on the door. Branson lost money, yet he got out before the other investors. In short, it could have been a whole lot worse. One of Branson's strengths in business is his timing—knowing when to enter a market, but also, just as important, when to get out.

How Branson handles setbacks is a large part of his success. His nickname, Dr. Yes, is telling: He is perpetually optimistic and will jump at new opportunities, which pushes him forward into businesses and markets where others would be cautious to tread. The flip side of such optimism, however, is that Branson occasionally plunges headfirst into a new business venture without doing sufficient market research. Overall, his gambles pay off, but as every gambler knows, even the best can get his fingers burned. Fortunately for Branson, Virgin's failures have not been (relatively speaking) capital intensive (unlike, for example, Virgin Atlantic) and have not had a detrimental impact on the overall reputation of the Virgin Group.

Branson has also been able to see the funny side of failure and, more often than not, turns the joke to his advantage. In 1985, Branson built the *Atlantic Challenger,* a boat he used to try to break the transatlantic crossing record and win the coveted Blue Riband for the fastest time. The *Challenger* sunk 300 miles off the British coast, and Branson and his crew had to be rescued, embarrassingly, by a banana boat. This could have been humiliating, but having just launched Virgin Atlantic, Branson rode high on the publicity generated by the sinking and took out a double-page advertisement in newspapers. Showing the hull of the boat sticking out of the water, the ad read, "Next time, Richard, take the plane." The public loved it, Virgin Atlantic's brand recognition increased substantially, and people saw it as a younger, cooler, more irreverent company than its competitors, which appealed to the airline's target market.

 Have a sense of humor about your failures to see them in a positive light.

Taxes

There is surprisingly little juicy gossip about Branson. He is a happily married father of two; he sits on the Global Drug Commission and avoids involvement in the drug industry (medical or recreational), so as not to lose his credibility as an impartial commissioner; and though he is open abut loving sex and uses innuendo and scantily clad female models to generate publicity for his products, there is not so much as a whiff of adultery, harassment, or abuse anywhere in his past. Much to his critics' frustration, Branson is pretty much squeaky-clean.

One issue that does rear its ugly head now and then, however, is Branson's personal tax evasion. In 2006, he was accused of moving to Necker, his private island in the British Virgin Islands, to avoid paying income taxes. Unlike U.S. tax law, which demands U.S. nationals and green-card holders pay their U.S. taxes from anywhere in the world, British nationals living overseas for more than 180 days a year do not pay tax to the British government. These "non-doms" (i.e., non-domiciled Brits) are within the law, but critics question the morality of their actions.

In Branson's case, even the morality aspect is not clear-cut: Branson has owned Necker since 1979 but lived and paid taxes in the U.K. for 40 years. His Virgin Group companies pay full taxes in the U.K. (unlike, for example, Starbucks, Google, and Vodafone, at whom the same criticisms have been levied), but

Branson has retired, more or less, to Necker, and his principal residence is indeed on the island. What's more, Branson claims that his personal earnings now go to charity, so even if he were still living in the U.K., he wouldn't be paying taxes on them.

As may be expected, Branson has paid no heed to these criticisms. As they have little impact on his bottom line, he has decided to focus on his businesses and personal projects rather than giving the tabloid accusations any air. He showed his ongoing love for the U.K. by posing in a (deliberately hideous) Union Jack suit on the Necker beach, another stunt that generated quite bit of press.

INFLUENCES AND AWARDS

Despite Branson's incredible public persona, we know relatively little about the man behind the mask. How does Branson see himself?

In a 2012 interview with *Entrepreneur* magazine, Branson let slip that his childhood hero was Peter Pan, the J.M. Barrie character who never gets old. Now well into his 60s, Branson shows no signs of slowing down: He has published another best-selling book, *The Virgin Way: How to Listen, Learn, Laugh, and Lead;* opened a new Virgin Hotel in Chicago; floated 15 percent of his stake in Virgin Money for £85 million; and made the groundbreaking (and press-generating) decision to grant his personal staff as much annual vacation time as they want, whenever they want. When asked whether aging is an advantage to entrepreneurs, Branson has been divided in his responses. He has said he values experience and is inspired by the likes of the Rolling Stones, who are still playing together after 50 years, yet he believes senior business leaders do get stuck in a rut of working with the same people. Branson stresses the importance of reaching out to the young, the energetic, and the imaginative, including by volunteering as a mentor, in order to keep your mind bright.

Who else has inspired Branson? His first answer is always Nelson Mandela, whom he has called "one of the most inspiring men I have ever met and had the honor to call my friend." Branson has read Mandela's autobiography, *Long Walk to Freedom,* many times over, and it was his close personal relationship with the South African president that gave birth to the Elders project in 2007.

Branson is an avid reader, and many books have had a profound effect on him. Al Gore's *An Inconvenient Truth* and James Lovelock's *The Revenge of Gaia* both developed his interest in ecological and humanitarian issues, and he reads historical titles, too, mentioning *Stalingrad: The Fateful Siege* by Antony Beevor and *Mao: The Unknown Story* by Jung Chang as particular favorites. He also loves reading comic books and founded Virgin Comics in 2006 in order to give "a whole generation of young creative thinkers a voice."

In anyone's book, Branson's achievements are remarkable, and he deserves a great deal of respect for having climbed from ordinary origins to become a multibillionaire in just 40 years. The honors and awards he has received demonstrate the impact he has had on people from all walks of life, as well as the legacy he will leave behind him. Branson was listed on the BBC's 2002 list of 100 Greatest Britons; in 2007 he was included in *Time* magazine's Top 100 Most Influential People in the World list; and in 2014 he was recognized by *The Sunday Times* as the most admired businessperson of the past five decades. He has received the Tony Jannus Award for accomplishments in commercial air transportation; the German Media Prize; the President's Merit Award for service to the music industry, from the National Academy of Recording Arts and Sciences; and the ISTA Prize from the International Space Transport Association for Virgin Galactic's development of suborbital transportation systems.

Though these accolades are undoubtedly significant, the awards Branson has received for his humanitarian work may mean the most to him. In 2007 UN Secretary-General Ban Ki-moon presented Branson with the United Nations Correspondents Association Citizen of the World Award for his support of environmental and humanitarian causes. This was followed in 2014 by the Business for Peace Award, given by the Business for Peace Foundation in Norway.

CONCLUSION

Branson's most famous book, his first biography, is titled *Losing My Virginity: How I Survived, Had Fun, and Made a Fortune Doing Business My Way*. In many aspects, the words of the title themselves sum up the man and his approach to business. The lessons we can learn from Branson are all contained there, so to conclude this chapter I'm going to break down that title into its component parts:

"Losing My Virginity"

Every one of us starts out in business like Branson, not knowing what we are going to do or how we are supposed to do it. Don't be put off by your own naïveté or inexperience. Recognize your shortcomings and be prepared to learn quickly, including learning from your own mistakes. If you don't jump into the deep end at some point, you will never learn to swim.

"How I Survived"

In the first few years of your new business, survival is the only thing that matters. You might not hit your targets or make money as quickly as you want, but if you hang in through the tough times, eventually you will find the opportunity that makes you a profit. If you always drop out too soon, you will never reach that point.

"Had Fun"

People buy into Branson and his brands because he looks as if he's always enjoying himself. Choose a business you are passionate about and want to get up in the morning to work on. Enthusiasm for your product motivates the team around you and tells customers unequivocally that they want some of what you have.

"Made a Fortune"

The endgame is making money, and you always need to keep this in mind. If something really isn't going to work, you have to be prepared to sacrifice it, however emotionally or financially attached to it you are, in order for something else to fly.

"Business My Way"

It is your business, so do it your way. If you copy what everyone else is already doing, you will never stand out from the crowd. Branson is a success because he does things differently from, and frequently better than, his competitors. Find your niche, or a novel approach, and make it your unique selling point.

Now all that remains is to kick-start your own business journey! In the words of Branson himself, "Screw it, let's do it." There's never a better time than now.

Warren Buffett

INTRODUCTION

In this chapter, you will learn the most significant skills and qualities that made Warren Buffett the most successful investor ever, along with some of his greatest investing tips. The best question to ask regarding Buffett is, Can financial and personal success be taught and passed down to others? The answer, of course, is yes—if you have the willingness to go beyond what is expected of you, to strive every day to be a better person, to take responsibility for all of your decisions whether they are good or bad, and not to view your failures as such but rather as lessons you can learn and profit from.

Buffett had a great many benefits that most people are not as lucky to have. He came from a long line of financial experts who made their fortunes buying and selling businesses and stocks, which in turn afforded him the chance to learn at the feet of great financial minds and attend top-notch schools that opened doors to prestigious investment firms and gave him the ability to grow his family fortune.

> "I think you are out of your mind if you keep taking jobs that you don't like because you think it will look good on your résumé. Isn't that a little like saving up sex for your old age?"
>
> —WARREN BUFFETT

But something else about Buffett sets him apart. Something beyond breeding, education, and business connections. It is something that cannot be taught and must be discovered: Buffett has been living his passion. In his iconic rise on the American financial scene, Buffett has proven time and again that passion breeds ingenuity, determination, and, ultimately, massive profits. Most people believe that they will never be able to live out their passion and that they will spend their days toiling away at jobs they hate, never taking time to discover their true path in life. Simply put, discovering your passion is a journey unto itself, and it is not easy.

THE START OF A PASSIONATE LIFE

Born in Omaha, Nebraska, on August 30, 1930, Warren Buffett was the middle child and only son of three children born to four-term congressman and stockbroker Howard Buffett and his wife, Leila. From an early age, Warren showed an exceptional aptitude with numbers, as well as a desire to make money. He entered the business world at the tender age of six by purchasing six-packs of Coca-Cola from his grandfather's grocery store for 25 cents and reselling them to his friends for five cents a bottle, making a five-cent profit per six-pack.

 It's never too early to find your passion.

While most of Buffett's friends spent their days playing games, he was learning the ins and outs of investing from his father and beginning to discover his passion for saving money and investing. Throughout his childhood, Buffett worked at his grandfather's grocery store, putting the money he had saved into his own small businesses, which included selling magazines door-to-door and candy and gum to his classmates.

Five years after these early forays into business, Buffett took his first tottering steps into the world of investment. At the age of 11, he purchased three shares of Cities Service Preferred stock at $38 a share for himself and his sister. Not long after, the stock price plummeted to $27 a share. Ever resilient, Buffett held onto his shares until they rebounded and increased to $40 a share, at which time he promptly sold them. The transaction ended up being a big mistake for the fledgling stockbroker, because the price later skyrocketed to $200 a share.

 When it comes to investing, as in life, patience is a virtue.

Perhaps the biggest mistake most novice investors, including the future Oracle of Omaha, make is to panic over losses, which is a huge detriment to building a strong and long-lasting portfolio. We all work hard for our money, and we want to see it grow and work hard for us. We want our investments to help us provide for our retirement, our children's education, our comfort and security. But what most beginning, and more than a few veteran, investors don't understand is that the stock market is a risk, and that with risk, you sometimes take losses. For many investors, taking a loss induces panic, and they toss out the offending stock like spoiled milk.

But just because an investment is falling in price doesn't mean you have to immediately abandon it. If we take a look at Buffett's legendary holding company, Berkshire Hathaway, a good deal of investors would have questioned the usefulness of some of his investment decisions: Coca-Cola, Geico insurance, Wrigley's gum. On paper, at least to the short-term thinker, these businesses would've looked like surefire losers when Buffett originally acquired them.

Buffett's true genius—the lesson he learned from his first investment—is that he recognizes what people want, need, and use, and what they will want, need, and use five, 10, and 20 years in the future. In order to make those judgments, you have to be patient as an investor and analyze the intrinsic value of a business and its long-term value in the marketplace. Yes, this can be a frightening way to invest, particularly for those who are betting their life savings on how well a handful of companies will do in the long run. But if you are patient and ride the ups and downs of a stock, you could have a winner that will set you up for life.

 ## Embrace the idea of short-term loss and long-term growth.

In 1947, at 17 years old, Buffett graduated from Woodrow Wilson High School in Washington, D.C., where his father was serving in the House of Representatives. Upon graduation, the younger Buffett originally had no intention of going to college. By this time, he had already made $5,000 delivering newspapers and through three pinball machines he had bought and placed in different local businesses. (Buffett eventually sold his pinball business for $1,200, the equivalent of around $50,000 in 2015 money.) But Buffett's education-oriented parents had other plans and pressured their only son to attend the Wharton School of Business at the University of Pennsylvania.

Buffett went reluctantly and stuck it out at Wharton for two years, often complaining that he knew more about business and investing than most of his professors did. When his father was defeated in his 1948 congressional reelection bid, Buffett returned to Omaha and transferred to the University of Nebraska–Lincoln. While a student there, he worked full-time at his father's investment brokerage and managed to graduate in only three years.

Buffett approached his graduate studies with the same stubbornness he had when he first entered college. His parents pressured him to apply to Harvard Business School. However, Harvard rejected the 20-year-old Buffett—a decision it surely regrets to this day—on the basis that he was too young. Stinging from this rejection, Buffett applied to the Columbia University School of Business, where renowned investor Ben Graham was teaching. Buffett's time at Columbia under Graham's wing proved formative.

> **"There seems to be some perverse human characteristic that likes to make easy things difficult."**
>
> —WARREN BUFFETT

MENTORS & COLLABORATORS

Throughout Buffett's long, storied career, he has always emphasized the need for continuing one's education—whether through conventional means, such as college, or more unconventional ones, like surrounding yourself with people you admire—and the need for elders to pass along their knowledge to younger generations.

Business and investing can seem like an intimidating labyrinth, and for the beginning investor or business owner, sometimes a wise, helping hand can be the single greatest assist a business can have. For most people, a mentor does not even have to be someone you actually know. A mentor can simply be someone whose ideas you identify with on a personal or professional level through articles, books, and television programs. Sometimes inspiration drawn from these distant, abstract relationships can drive you forward in setting and accomplishing the goals you create for yourself.

The need for a mentor in business—
or any endeavor, really—is vital.

Buffett benefited from the sage advice of two of the most brilliant business minds of the 20th century: his teacher Ben Graham, an investor and Geico insurance chairman; and Charlie Munger, Buffett's longtime partner in Berkshire Hathaway.

Ben Graham

In the 1920s, stockbroker Ben Graham became well known in many business circles as a shrewd, calculating, and aggressive investor. During a period when most investors approached the stock market as something of a crap shoot, Graham sought out stocks that were so radically undervalued they were considered practically devoid of risk—and, in the eyes of most investors, any real growth.

One of Graham's best-known investments was in the Northern Pipeline, an oil transportation company managed by the Rockefeller family. Shares were trading at around $60, but after analyzing an annual balance sheet, Graham realized the company had bond holdings worth $95 for each share. He failed to convince its management to sell the portfolio, so Graham waged a proxy war and secured a spot on the board of directors. Northern sold its bonds and was able to pay a dividend of $70 per share.

At the age of 40, Graham published what is widely considered one the cornerstones of modern investment literature, *Security Analysis.* At the time of its publication, investing in the stock market was considered extremely risky, and investing in equities futures had become something of a joke, with the Dow short several years after the stock-market crash of 1929. Graham introduced the principle of intrinsic business value, a means of measuring the true value of a business totally independent of its stock offering. Using intrinsic value, investors could decide what a company was worth and make investment decisions accordingly. Buffett characterized Graham's subsequent book, *The Intelligent Investor*, as the greatest book on investing ever written.

During his graduate business studies at Columbia, Buffett was the only student ever to earn an A+ in one of Graham's classes. After graduation, Buffett was set on becoming a full-time stockbroker on Wall Street, but both his father and Graham advised him against it. Buffett was so determined to work on Wall Street, however, he offered to work for Graham's investment firm for free. Graham turned him down. Not being able to work for his friend and mentor was crushing, and Buffett returned home to Nebraska to once again work at his father's firm.

Charlie Munger

After he left New York, it would be more than another ten years before Buffett met the man who would become his lifelong business partner and right-hand man at Berkshire Hathaway, the enigmatic Charlie Munger. Like Buffett, Munger was originally from Omaha. After a brief period of studying mathematics at the University of Michigan, Munger dropped out of college to serve as a meteorologist in the U.S. Army Air Corps during World War II. After the war, Munger began studying law at Caltech before entering Harvard Law School without an undergraduate degree. He graduated from Harvard in 1948 and moved with his family to California, where he began practicing law with the firm Wright & Garrett.

In 1962, Munger moved back to Omaha. When mutual friends introduced the future partners, Buffett initially found Munger somewhat snobbish and a bit off-putting, but he soon came to recognize Munger's financial and legal brilliance, and the two drew closer.

EARLY EXPERIMENTS

After taking a job at his father's brokerage firm, Buffett began dating a young woman named Susie Thompson. Within a few years, their relationship turned serious and in April 1952, they were married. They rented a three-room apartment for $65 a month. The apartment was run-down and home to several mice. It was here that their daughter, also named Susie, was born. In order to save money, they made a bed for her in a dresser drawer.

During these years, Buffett's investments were largely limited to a gas station and unfruitful real estate deals. None were successful. However, during this time Buffet began teaching night courses at the University of Omaha, something that would not have been possible for the naturally shy young man if not for a Dale Carnegie public-speaking course, a class Buffett still credits as being the most beneficial to his professional life.

 Do not underestimate the power of being able to speak for yourself.

Despite the financial obstacles of Buffett's early career, things began to look up when he received a call from his old mentor, Graham, who finally invited the young stockbroker to join his New York brokerage firm. The Buffetts purchased a home in the New York suburbs, and Warren spent his days analyzing Standard & Poors reports and seeking out investment opportunities. During this early period at Graham Partnerships, the differences between Buffett's and Graham's financial philosophies began to surface.

Buffett became interested in how companies worked, specifically in what made certain companies superior to their competitors. Graham simply wanted the cold, hard numbers. Whereas

Buffett was far more interested in a company's management style and workforce as major factors in deciding when to invest, Graham looked mainly at balance sheets and income statements and could care less about corporate management and leadership.

During his time at Graham Partnerships, from 1950 to 1956, Buffett built his personal capital up to $140,000 from an initial $9,800 in personal assets. With this fortune, Buffett decided to leave Graham Partnerships and return to Omaha to plan his next big move. On May 1, 1956, shortly after returning home, Buffett recruited seven limited partners—including his aunt and older sister—and raised an extra $100,000 in capital. With only $100 he had put in himself, he officially created Buffett Associates, Ltd.

Within a year, he was managing more than $300,000 in capital. In the same year, he and Susie purchased a home they affectionately nicknamed Buffett's Folly (Buffett still occupies it, at least part-time, to this day). He managed the partnership from the master bedroom, later moving the operation to a small office. Buffett's life in Omaha was finally beginning to take shape. He was married to a lovely woman, he had three adoring children, and he was running his first very successful holding company.

Over the next five years, Buffett Associates generated an impressive 250 percent profit per year. Even more impressive, the company was seeing massive returns while the Dow was uncharacteristically low. Buffett's success was making him something of a celebrity around Omaha. By 1962, Buffett Partnership had capital in excess of $7.5 million, $1 million of which was Buffett's personal stake in the fund, which in turn made him a majority owner. He also made more than 90 limited partnerships available to investors across the country. In one decisive move, he grouped the partnerships into a single entity, renamed the company Buffett Partnerships Ltd., increased the minimum investment in the holding company to $100,000, and opened an office in Omaha.

A decade after its founding, Buffett Partnerships was seeing record-breaking profits with assets generating more than a

1,000 percent return over the course of a decade. By 1967, it had grown to an amazing $45 million dollars, with Buffett's personal stake being around $7 million. In 1968, Buffett closed the partnership to new accounts, and the company saw its largest gain, recording a nearly 60 percent increase in profits as the Dow fluctuated wildly due to the Vietnam War. Buffett's personal fortune swelled to more than $100 million in assets.

Because of his connections and his family's renown, Buffett was able to easily find investors and partners in his early ventures. Without these partners, chances are he would never have gotten his businesses off the ground. True, he could simply have invested his own capital, but this would have limited his overall amount of investment dollars, and only he would have benefited, as opposed to creating vast amounts of wealth for his investors.

> "I insist on a lot of time being spent, almost every day, to just sit and think. That is very uncommon in American business. I read and think. So I do more reading and thinking, and make less impulse decisions, than most people in business. I do it because I like this kind of life."
>
> —Warren Buffett

Creating a business, particularly in a struggling economy, can seem like an almost impossible feat. But when you have a good idea and a solid business plan in place, you would be surprised by the number of people who are willing to get in on the ground floor, particularly family members and friends. Buffett most likely offered partnerships to his family members first because they knew him best and believed he had the education and know-how to make their initial money grow into the fortune it eventually became.

So does this mean you should hit Mom and Dad up for a loan to open your first business? Absolutely not! To many, your idea may seem risky (maybe even to you), and they may be reluctant to enter into a business venture where they may lose their initial investment or not see a return on it for many years. This is why it's absolutely vital that you create a solid business plan before you actually approach anyone about investing in a business opportunity. Even if you go the more conventional route of approaching a bank for a small-business loan, it will want to see solid, convincing documentation that your idea will make money and that the loan will be paid back in a timely manner.

 Before asking anyone to invest in you, prove your dedication with a solid business plan.

So if you have what you think is a zero-failure idea (but what idea or plan is really zero failure?), plan ahead. In fact, plan very far ahead—as much as a decade, if you can—because this will be very effective in convincing investors how serious you are in pursuing your passion. Also let potential investors know you are willing to risk just as much capital as they are by trying to match their initial investment. For most people, this will take a bit of saving. If you're trying to entice potential investors, you don't also want the responsibility of paying back a bank loan as well. But if you have passion, drive, and ambition, you should have no problem cutting a few financial corners to help you save for your seed money.

Most important, don't give up! If you are truly passionate about your business plan, you will find a way to make it happen, even if you have to work three jobs and operate on zero sleep to do so.

221

BERKSHIRE HATHAWAY

In 1969, at the peak of the Vietnam War, a period that saw the Dow balloon and stock prices rise to unprecedented heights, Buffett began to liquidate the partnership. In May of that year, he informed his partners that he was "unable to find any bargains in the current market" and spent the remainder of the year liquidating the portfolio except for two companies: Berkshire Hathaway and Diversified Retailing.

Shares of Berkshire Hathaway were distributed among the partners, with a letter from Buffett informing them that he would be involved with Berkshire in some capacity but was under no obligation to them in the future. Warren was clear in his intention to hold onto his own stake in the company—he was a majority owner, holding a 29 percent stake—but he did not reveal his intentions for the company or what role he would play in it.

His role at Berkshire, however, had actually been defined years earlier. In 1965, after accumulating 49 percent of the company's common stock, Buffett named himself director. Poor management had run the flagging holding company nearly into the ground, and he was certain with a bit of tweaking, it could be run better and begin generating a profit. Buffett made Ken Chace president, giving him complete autonomy. Although he refused to award stock options because he considered it unfair to shareholders, he did agree to cosign for a loan of nearly $20,000 so that Chace could purchase 1,000 shares of Berkshire Hathaway stock.

Two years later, in 1967, Buffett met with Berkshire's controlling shareholder, Jack Ringwalt, and asked what he thought the company was worth. Ringwalt told Buffett at least $50 per share, which was at a $17 premium above its then trading price of $33. Buffett offered to buy the whole company on the spot, a move that cost him $8.6 million dollars. That same year,

Berkshire paid out a dividend of 10 cents on its outstanding stock, something that would never happen again. Years later, Buffett joked that he must have been in the bathroom when the dividend was declared.

In 1970, Buffett named himself chairman of the board of Berkshire Hathaway, and his capital allocation soon began to display his prudence; textile profits were a pitiful $45,000, while insurance and banking each brought in $2.1 and $2.6 million dollars. The paltry cash brought in from the struggling looms in New Bedford, Massachusetts, had provided the stream of capital necessary to start building Berkshire Hathaway.

A year or so later, Buffett was offered the chance to buy the California-based company See's Candy, a gourmet chocolate maker that sold its products at a premium. The balance sheet reflected what Californians already knew: They were more than willing to pay a bit more for the special See's taste. Buffett decided Berkshire would purchase the company for $25 million in cash. The See's owners held out for $30 million but quickly conceded. It was the largest acquisition Berkshire Hathaway, or Buffett himself, had ever made.

After the successful See's Candy acquisition, Buffett attempted to merge Berkshire with industrial giant Wesco, which prompted an SEC investigation that ultimately caused the merger to fail. Buffett and Munger had offered to buy Wesco stock at a highly inflated price simply because they thought it was "the right thing to do." Unsurprisingly, the government didn't believe them, and the merger was denied.

But Buffett began to see Berkshire Hathaway's net worth climb. From 1965 to 1975, the company's value rose from $20 per share to almost $100. Also during this period, Buffett made his final purchases of Berkshire stock. He had invested more than $15.4 million dollars into the company at an average cost of $32.45 per share—bringing his ownership to more than 43 percent of the stock, with Susie Buffett holding another

3 percent. His entire net worth was in Berkshire Hathaway. With no personal holdings, Buffett made the company his sole investment vehicle.

In 1976, Buffett again became involved with the Geico insurance company, which had recently reported amazingly high losses; its stock was trading at only $2 per share. Buffett wisely realized that the basic business was still intact and that most of the problems Geico was facing were caused by inept management. Over the next several years, Berkshire built up its position on this ailing insurer and reaped millions in profits. Graham, who still held his fortune in the company, died shortly before the turnaround. Years later, the insurance giant would become a fully owned subsidiary of Berkshire Hathaway.

> "Rule No. 1: Never lose money.
> Rule No. 2: Never forget Rule No. 1."
>
> —WARREN BUFFETT

By the late '70s, Buffett's reputation was so great that if there was even a rumor that he was buying a stock, it was enough to shoot the price up 10 percent. Berkshire Hathaway's stock was trading at more than $290 a share, and Buffett's personal wealth was almost $140 million. The irony was that he never sold a single share of Berkshire, meaning his entire available cash was the $50,000 salary he received as chairman. At the time, he made the offhanded comment to a broker, "Everything I got is tied up in Berkshire. I'd like a few nickels outside."

This prompted Buffett to start investing for his personal life, and he was far more speculative with his own investments. At one point, he bought copper futures, an act of unadulterated speculation that was viewed in the investment world as entirely a crapshoot, but in only nine months, he made $3 million dollars on it. When a friend prompted him to invest in real estate,

Buffett responded, "Why should I buy real estate when the stock market is so easy?"

 Don't be afraid to go against the trends if you really believe in your strategy.

For all the fine businesses Berkshire Hathaway had managed to collect, one of its best and most profitable was just about to come into its stable. In 1983, Buffett walked into Nebraska Furniture Mart, a multimillion-dollar retailer built from the ground up by Rose Blumpkin. Speaking to the owner, Buffett asked if she would be interested in selling the store to Berkshire. Her answer was a simple yes, that she would part with her business for $60 million. The deal was sealed on a handshake, and a single-page contract was drawn up. Blumpkin, a Russian-born immigrant, merely folded the check without looking at it when she received it days later in the mail.

In 1986, the Scott & Fetzer vacuum-cleaner company proved another great addition to the Berkshire family. It had been the target of a hostile takeover when its chairman, Ralph Schey, launched a leveraged buyout in 1984. Investor Ivan Boesky made a counter offer for $60 a share—the original tender offer stood at $50, which was $5 above market value. Scott & Fetzer, needless to say, was panicking. Buffett, who owned a quarter of a million shares, sent a message to the company asking them to call if they were interested in a merger. The phone rang almost immediately. Berkshire offered $60 per share in cold, hard cash. When the deal was wrapped up less than a week later, Berkshire had a new $315 million–dollar cash-generating powerhouse to add to its collection.

In 1986, Buffett discovered a new passion when he bought a used Falcon aircraft for $850,000. As his face had become increasingly recognizable, he was no longer comfortable flying commercial. This kind of luxury was hard for him to adjust to, but he loved the jet immensely, and his passion eventually led him to purchase the Executive Jet company in the mid-1990s.

Berkshire Hathaway continued to increase in value through the 1980s, except for one noisy, destructive bump in the road: the stock-market crash of 1987, a.k.a. Black Monday. Buffett wasn't upset about the market correction; he calmly checked the price of his company and went back to work. This was representative of how he viewed stocks and businesses in general. This was one of the stock market's temporary aberrations, albeit quite a strong one—nearly one quarter of Berkshire's market capital was wiped out. Seemingly unfazed by the losses, Buffett and his company powered through the devastation.

> **"It is not necessary to do extraordinary things to get extraordinary results."**
>
> —Warren Buffett

A year later, Buffett started buying up Coca-Cola stock. The president of Coca-Cola noticed someone was loading up on shares and became concerned. After researching the transactions, he found the trades were being placed from the Midwest. He immediately thought of Buffett and telephoned him. Buffett confessed to being the culprit and requested that they not speak of it until he was legally required to disclose his holdings, at the 5 percent threshold. Within a few months, Berkshire owned 7 percent of the company, or $1.02 billion dollars' worth of the stock. Within three years, Buffett's Coca-Cola stock would be worth more than the entire value of Berkshire had been when he made the investment.

By 1989, Berkshire Hathaway was trading at $8,000 a share, and Buffett was personally worth more than $3.8 billion dollars. In the next ten years, he would be worth ten times that amount.

During the rest of the 1990s, Berkshire Hathaway's stock cata-pulted as high as $80,000 per share. Even with this astronomi-cal feat, Buffett was accused of losing his touch as the dot-com frenzy took hold. In 1999, when Berkshire reported a net increase of 0.5 percent per share, several newspapers ran stories about the demise of the Wizard of Omaha.

Confident the technology bubble would burst, Buffett contin-ued to do what he did best: allocate capital into great businesses that were selling below intrinsic value. His efforts did not go unre-warded. When the markets finally did come to their senses, he was once again a star. Berkshire's stock recovered to its previous levels after falling to around $45,000 per share and then rebounding to around $75,000 a share. Buffett was once again held in high regard.

After the turn of the millennium, Buffett continued to pur-chase companies that he liked because of their successful busi-ness models and their long histories on the American scene. Most notably, he purchased controlling shares for Berkshire Hathaway of Wrigley's, Nestlé, and Heinz. His reasoning behind each of the purchases was simple enough: He liked the taste of their products. Certainly other factors were involved, such as solid and consistent returns, but keeping his response so whim-sical made for far better newspaper copy.

MAKING THE WORLD A BETTER PLACE

Perhaps the most amazing thing about Buffett is that despite being one of the wealthiest men in the world, he is also one of the most generous. He has decided to make the world a better place in his lifetime. Every day for more than 30 years, he has striven to set an example among his peers.

In 1981, at the start of the decade of greed, Berkshire announced a new charity plan that was thought up by Munger and approved by Buffett. It called for each shareholder to designate charities that would receive $2 for each Berkshire share the stockholder owned. This was in response to a common practice on Wall Street of the CEO choosing who received the company's handouts—often they would go to the executive's school, church, or organizations. The plan was a huge success, and over the years the amount was upped for each share.

 Innovation doesn't stop with your own interests—find new ways to help others.

At its peak, Berkshire shareholders were giving away millions of dollars each year, all to their own causes. The program was eventually discontinued, after associates at one of Berkshire's subsidiaries, the Pampered Chef, experienced discrimination because of the controversial pro-choice charities Buffett had chosen to allocate his prorated portion of the charitable contribution pool.

In 2006, Buffet pledged the bulk of his fortune to the Bill & Melinda Gates foundation, which in turn sparked the Giving Pledge. The new organization started by Buffet and Bill Gates aimed to recruit the wealthiest 1 percent of Americans to give away at least half their personal fortunes upon their death or before.

Buffett has stipulated in his will that he will give his children and grandchildren only enough money to discover their own passions, while the rest of his fortune is to go to the Bill & Melinda Gates Foundation, whence the couple can put it toward any cause they see fit. This level of generosity and forethought is truly inspiring, and it cannot help but get you thinking about how you will leave the world when you die. What kind of mark have you made upon the planet and on your fellow human beings? What do you do right now that affects those around you?

Most of us will never be able to leave behind the kind of legacy Buffett has, but we can take his cue and start attempting to change the world in small ways. Perhaps the most effective is to simply volunteer our time to causes we believe in. Give an hour or two of time a month at a homeless shelter, a local school, or anywhere human resources are in short supply. This may seem to be a great effort because all of us lead busy lives. Between work and family obligations, there doesn't even seem to be enough time in the day to properly eat and rest. But if you really take a look at your schedule, chances are there is time to go out and help your community. If you really think about it, how much time do you waste each day doing things like watching television or spending time on the internet? Chances are you spend days doing nothing but relaxing.

And volunteering doesn't always have to focus on those who are less fortunate. If you look at your community, how many different activities are available to children? Are there sports leagues in need of coaches? Are there adult education classes that need tutors for students who are struggling to learn a new skill? These are things you can give a small amount of time to and actually change the world through your efforts. Volunteering to be a soccer coach isn't as dramatic as donating billions that will go toward curing diseases or building new schools, but it will create positive change for the individuals you're helping, and this, hopefully, will in turn inspire those people you've reached out to, and they'll want to help others as well.

 Volunteering is a great way to pay it forward.

But if all this seems like too much on your plate, look to your own home instead. Are there small ways you can effect change right from your couch at the end of the day? Chances are the answer is yes, and they're probably sitting right in front of you. Look to your family, children, and spouse, and think about what you do that affects them in a positive manner. What lessons are you teaching them that will help them better the world? Will they go on to greater things than you have accomplished? Are you acting as a positive role model in their upbringing to ensure their success in the world?

Yes, these things are by no means grandiose in scale, but small actions can very well lead to a far brighter future for everyone if we simply show an effort and try to change the world.

CHALLENGES AND TRIALS

Like the rest of us, Buffett has faced his fair share of personal and business crises. What sets him apart from others when faced with a crisis is his ability to logically assess situations and not allow them to physically and emotionally shock him or disrupt his day-to-day existence. And although most of Buffett's life has been blessed with more than his fair share of good fortune, as with every success story, there are periods where a person is tested to almost beyond his or her limits. Buffett is no exception and has faced levels of adversity that would break most people.

 Don't abandon logic when faced with a crisis. Keep your head.

The Death of Susie Buffett

In 1977 at the age of 45, Susie Buffett left her husband. Although they remained married, she wished to pursue a career as a singer and moved alone to an apartment in San Francisco to do so. Warren was devastated. Despite the separation, he and Susie remained close, speaking every day, taking their annual two-week New York trip together, and meeting the kids at their California beach house for Christmas celebrations. The transition was hard for Warren, but he eventually grew somewhat accustomed to the new arrangement. Susie called several women in the Omaha area and insisted they go to dinner and a movie with her husband. Eventually, she introduced Warren to a waitress named Astrid Menks. Within the year, Astrid had moved in with him at Buffett's Folly with Susie's blessing, and the two have been together ever since.

> "It takes 20 years to build a reputation and five minutes to ruin it. If you think about that, you'll do things differently."
>
> —WARREN BUFFETT

In 2003, Susie was diagnosed with oral cancer and underwent surgery, radiation treatments, and facial reconstruction due to bone loss. Warren made it a point to fly out to her home every weekend during this long, painful period. Just as it looked as if Susie would fully recover from the cancer, she suffered a cerebral hemorrhage and died at the age of 82. Warren was by her side when she passed and was so devastated by her loss that he was unable to attend her memorial service.

The Salomon Brothers Scandal

In 1991, U.S. Treasury Deputy Assistant Secretary Mike Basham learned that Salomon Brothers trader Paul Mozer had been submitting false bids between December 1990 and May 1991 in an attempt to purchase more Treasury bonds than were permitted by one buyer. Salomon was fined $290 million for this infraction, the largest fine ever levied on an investment bank at the time. Soon afterward, Buffett was brought in to take over the day-to-day operations of Salomon Brothers, a firm that Berkshire Hathaway held a partial stake in and that Buffett held a personal, yet entirely passive, investment in as well. He was tasked with stripping the struggling brokerage of its untoward elements and finding a buyer for the firm.

Buffett described the period in which he ran Salomon Brothers as one of the most stressful in his long career because of the external pressures of SEC investigators, the internal strife and disorganization of Salomon's management team, and the issues the firm faced in its public offering of MCI Communications. But within a year, Buffett found a buyer: the Travelers Group. The Salomon CEO was forced out in August 1991 and an SEC settlement resulted in a fine of $100,000; the CEO was banned from serving as the chief executive of a brokerage firm. The scandal was documented in the 1993 book *Nightmare on Wall Street.*

Gen Re & AIG

In October 2000, some Wall Street analysts and SEC investigators questioned the decline in American International Group (AIG) loss reserves. In an effort to quell these concerns, AIG entered into two sham reinsurance transactions with Cologne Reinsurance Dublin, a subsidiary of General Reinsurance; they had no economic substance but were designed to add $500 million in phony loss reserves to AIG's balance sheet in the fourth quarter of 2000 and first quarter of 2001.

In 2005, New York attorney general Eliot Spitzer began an investigation into the two transactions. Soon afterward, AIG came under market pressure and admitted it had undertaken what could be construed as securities fraud. The staff said the reinsurance transactions had inflated AIG's balance sheet and propped up its stock price. In the resulting stock crash, investors lost $500 million. General Reinsurance, more commonly known as Gen Re, was a wholly owned subsidiary of Berkshire Hathaway, and Buffett was called to a New York grand jury and in front of Congress to detail his involvement with both Gen Re and AIG. Buffett had faced federal scrutiny before, as well as investigations from the SEC, but he had never been involved in a scandal as big as this one.

Despite the seriousness of the allegations and the overall threat to Berkshire's stability, Buffett kept his cool and affable demeanor throughout the hearings, answering every question thrown at him with his trademark intelligence and good humor. By the end of it, Buffett and Berkshire walked away fairly unscathed, but the hearings themselves were far reaching, and many new protections were put into place to make sure that firms cannot create such oversights in the future.

> **"The most important thing to do if you find yourself in a hole is to stop digging."**
>
> —WARREN BUFFETT

How do you react when faced with adversity? Do you run and hide from it, emotionally shutting yourself down in hopes that it will just disappear if you're quiet and meek enough? Or do you face it head-on and take responsibility for your actions? In certain circumstances, adversity and strife are unavoidable. When faced with the long-term illness or death of a loved one, this kind of adversity is beyond painful, and all we can really do is live through it.

But what about other types of adversity, such as work assignments or the occasional fights you have with your spouse or friends? Do you oftentimes find yourself feeling overwhelmed and cowering from confrontation or extra responsibility? Do you try to shift blame onto others or simply shirk putting the necessary extra effort into your endeavors? In the adverse situations Buffett faced, he remained clearheaded and rational. He knew that if he did not face his and his company's issues head-on, chances were they would ultimately come back to haunt him and hurt his business.

CONCLUSION

What has set Buffett apart from most investors is his willingness to soldier on in his work no matter the amount of adversity or personal difficulties he faces. Work has been his solace, his escape. While many of us retreat and run from our problems, Buffett has tackled his challenges and always seems to profit from his straightforward approach to business and life.

With the housing crash and great recession of 2008, Buffett and Berkshire Hathaway went through the same amount of turmoil as most investment firms and holding companies did. But because of the sound, proven investments in their portfolio and Buffett's complete lack of interest in real estate, real estate holding companies, and mortgage futures, Berkshire and Buffett came out of the Great Recession fairly unscathed. Of course, like most stock portfolios, Berkshire Hathaway's did suffer a devaluation. But at that point in Buffett's long life and career, the loss of capital was a minor one, which he saw as simply another fluctuation in a long history of them.

On February 15, 2011, Buffett was awarded the Presidential Medal of Freedom by President Barack Obama. Buffet himself had been a huge supporter of Obama's campaign in 2008, but in his 80s, Buffett has mostly concerned himself with the Giving Pledge charity and various speaking engagements at colleges and corporations around the world. Although he still chairs the annual Berkshire investors' meeting, he now allows others to pilot the daily operations of this iconic holding company.

What Buffett's life can teach us is that a life of passion is also a life of obsession; the two walk hand in hand. When you live this kind of life, there are no limits. There are no time clocks, no vacations, no bosses breathing down your neck, because with obsession, there is no boss, there is only you and your obsession and your desire to work on it day after day to perfect it and make it fully your own. This kind of passion and obsession does not happen overnight. Some people, like Buffett, simply seem to be born with a clear idea of what they want and how to accomplish it. But for most, it takes time for a passion to emerge and set you down your chosen path.

If you have found your passion—the thing that makes you jump out of bed every day, eager for it to start and disappointed when it comes to a close because you feel you have so much more to do—count yourself lucky, because you are a rarity. Living a life of passion may feel like a burden at times due to various roadblocks or limitations, but if you remain persistent and stay true to yourself, your passion, and your vision of your future and career, eventually you will be doing exactly what you want.

For those of you who have yet to discover what drives you, don't give up. Never stop looking, and stay curious and focused. Read, give yourself time to sit and think, experience life, and pursue your education, whether in a college classroom or the classroom of experience. If you remain curious, there's a better chance that you will eventually discover your passion.

But if for some reason it doesn't happen, don't be disheartened. Sometimes passion emerges only through effort—effort at your job, effort as a spouse and parent, effort in your hobbies and interests. The point is to constantly strive to make yourself a better person who cares deeply and passionately about family, friends, work, life, and the eventual achievement all of your goals. By doing this, by living every moment as if it were your last, you will be living the Warren Buffett way.